CHRISTMAS

IS

COOKIES

and Gingerbread and Spice Cake and Fudge and More

TIME
LIFE
CUSTOM
PUBLISHING

TIME-LIFE BOOKS, ALEXANDRIA, VIRGINIA

TIME-LIFE BOOKS IS A DIVISION OF TIME LIFE INC.

TIME-LIFE CUSTOM PUBLISHING

VICE PRESIDENT and PUBLISHER	Terry Newell
Project Manager	Teresa Graham
Director of Sales	Neil Levin
Director of New Product Development	Regina Hall
Managing Editor	Donia Ann Steele
Retail Promotions Manager	Gary Stoiber
Production Manager	Carolyn Mills Bounds
Quality Assurance Manager	Miriam P. Newton

Produced by Rebus, Inc.
New York, New York

Illustrations
William Neeper

Library of Congress Cataloging-in-Publication Data
Christmas is cookies and gingerbread and spice cake and fudge and more
/ the editors of Time-Life Books.
p. cm. -- (The everyday cookbooks)
Includes index.
ISBN 0-7835-4824-9
ISBN 0-7835-4827-3
1. Christmas cookery. 2. Confectionery. 3. Cookery, International.
I. Time-Life Books. II. Series.
TX739.2.C45C464   1996
641.5'68--dc20   96-271
                                                                    CIP

Books produced by Time-Life Custom Publishing are available
at special bulk discount for promotional and premium use.
Custom adaptations can also be created to meet
your specific marketing goals.
Call 1-800-323-5255.

Introduction

Remember the wonderful flavors and aromas of grandma's kitchen? The following pages are fairly bursting with homespun recipes that recall the happy holidays of childhood. Here are sweet treats with the mouth-watering goodness of bakeshop classics, from favorites like Sugar Cookie Cut-Outs and Snickerdoodles to festive delights like Plum Pudding and Pfeffernüsse. In this gala assortment of holiday confections, you'll find time-honored, beloved classics such as Boston Cream Pie and Cranberry-Almond Bread, along with exciting new twists like Brownie Cheesecake Bars and White Chocolate Truffles.

Christmas Is Cookies is a baking bonanza, with over 100 easy-to-follow recipes for cookies and bars, cakes, pies and puddings, candy, quick breads and coffee cakes. These desserts run the gamut of size, shape, design, and texture: Try crisp or chewy, monster or mini, pretzel-shaped or pinwheeled, round or rectangular. The pages are sprinkled with notes on simple variations and substitutions to expand your options.

Christmas is a time of hospitality, and homemade desserts are perfect as treats for guests or as gifts for anyone on your list. This is a collection of recipes that will bring back fond memories and put everyone in the holiday spirit. Yet these sweet treats are not just for Christmas; old-fashioned flavors and simple ingredients hold a wealth of good cheer that is always in season.

Baking is an infinitely satisfying and comforting pastime. So bake a batch of cookies as a gesture of love—and prove life *is* sweet.

—Mara Reid Rogers,
author of numerous cookbooks
and spokesperson for <u>The Everyday Cookbooks</u>™.

Contents

PIES & PUDDINGS

CANDY

QUICK BREADS & COFFEE CAKES

INDEX

COOKIES & BARS

Gingerbread Men

MAKES 2 DOZEN

⅓ CUP MOLASSES

½ CUP LIGHT BROWN SUGAR

1 TABLESPOON GROUND GINGER

½ TEASPOON CINNAMON

½ TEASPOON GROUND CLOVES

½ TEASPOON NUTMEG

½ TEASPOON BAKING SODA

1 STICK BUTTER, CUT INTO PIECES

1 EGG, LIGHTLY BEATEN

2½ CUPS FLOUR

¼ TEASPOON BAKING POWDER

¼ TEASPOON SALT

1¼ CUPS POWDERED SUGAR

2 TABLESPOONS WATER

¼ TEASPOON VANILLA EXTRACT

DRIED FRUITS, CUT INTO SMALL PIECES

1. Preheat the oven to 325°. Lightly grease a baking sheet.

2. In a medium saucepan, bring the molasses, brown sugar, ginger, cinnamon, cloves, and nutmeg to a low boil, stirring occasionally. Add the baking soda and stir until the mixture foams up in the saucepan, 1 to 2 minutes.

3. Place the butter pieces in a large bowl. Pour the hot molasses mixture over the butter and stir to melt the butter. Add the egg and stir to blend. Gradually stir in the flour, baking powder, and salt.

4. Turn the dough out onto a lightly floured surface and knead it lightly until the dough is smooth; form it into a ball. Roll the dough out to a ¼-inch thickness.

5. Cut out the cookies using floured cookie cutters. Place the cookies on the prepared baking sheet, about 1 inch apart. Gather, reroll, and cut the remaining scraps of dough. Bake the cookies for 13 to 15 minutes, or until crisp.

6. Let the cookies cool on the baking sheet for 2 to 3 minutes, then transfer them to a rack to cool completely.

7. Meanwhile, in a small bowl, combine the powdered sugar, water, and vanilla, and stir until thick and smooth; set the icing aside.

8. Fill a pastry bag with the icing and pipe it onto the cookies. Add details with bits of the dried fruits.

SUGAR COOKIE CUT-OUTS

MAKES 2 DOZEN

2 STICKS BUTTER, AT ROOM
TEMPERATURE
¾ CUP SUGAR
3 EGG YOLKS

½ TEASPOON VANILLA EXTRACT
¼ TEASPOON ALMOND EXTRACT
2½ CUPS FLOUR
RED AND GREEN COLORED SUGAR

1. Preheat the oven to 375°. Lightly grease a baking sheet.

2. In a large bowl, cream the butter and sugar until light and fluffy. Beat in the egg yolks, 1 at a time, until well incorporated. Beat in the vanilla and almond extracts. Gradually beat in 1½ cups of the flour, then form the dough into a ball.

3. Transfer the dough to a lightly floured surface, and knead in the remaining cup of flour until all of the flour is incorporated and the dough is smooth. Roll it out into a rough circle about ⅛ inch thick. With your choice of Christmas cookie cutters, cut out as many cookies as you can. Gather together all the scraps, roll out the dough again, and cut out additional cookies. Repeat until you have used all of the dough.

4. Place the cookies 1 inch apart on the prepared baking sheet and sprinkle with colored sugar. Bake for 8 minutes, or until the cookies are golden. Transfer the cookies to racks to cool.

VARIATION: *Dress up the cookies with decorator's icing: Stir together 1 cup sifted powdered sugar, ½ teaspoon vanilla extract, a pinch of salt, and enough water or half-and-half (1 to 2 tablespoons) to create a spreadable consistency. Pipe designs on the cookies with a decorating tube, or spread the icing on the cookies with a small spatula and top it with colored sugar or sprinkles.*

Saint Nicholas Spice Cookies

MAKES 6 DOZEN

2 TO 2¼ CUPS FLOUR

1 TABLESPOON CINNAMON

½ TEASPOON GROUND MACE

½ TEASPOON GROUND ANISE SEEDS

¼ TEASPOON GROUND GINGER

¼ TEASPOON NUTMEG

¼ TEASPOON GROUND CLOVES

¼ TEASPOON BAKING POWDER

⅛ TEASPOON SALT

1½ STICKS BUTTER, AT ROOM
 TEMPERATURE

1 CUP LIGHT BROWN SUGAR

3 TABLESPOONS MILK

1½ CUPS SLICED ALMONDS

1. Preheat the oven to 375°. Lightly grease 2 large baking sheets.

2. In a medium bowl, combine 2 cups of the flour, the cinnamon, mace, anise, ginger, nutmeg, cloves, baking powder, and salt; set aside.

3. In a large bowl, cream the butter and sugar until light and fluffy. Beat in the milk a tablespoon at a time, then add the flour mixture ½ cup at a time, beating well after each addition. When finished the dough should be firm enough to gather into a compact ball; if necessary, add up to ¼ cup more flour by the tablespoonful. Or, if the dough is too stiff to beat easily, knead in the remaining flour mixture with your hands.

4. Roll out the dough between 2 sheets of wax paper until it is about ⅛ inch thick. Gently pull away the top sheet of wax paper and, with a pastry wheel or sharp knife, cut the dough into 1½ x 2½-inch rectangles. Press the almonds gently into the cookies, dividing the nuts evenly among them. Refrigerate the cookies for about 30 minutes, then transfer them from the bottom sheet of wax paper to the prepared baking sheets.

5. Bake for 8 to 10 minutes, or until brown and firm. Let the cookies cool to room temperature before removing them from the baking sheets.

CANDY CANE COOKIES

MAKES 4 DOZEN

2½ CUPS FLOUR

1 TEASPOON SALT

2 STICKS BUTTER, AT ROOM
  TEMPERATURE

1 CUP POWDERED SUGAR

1 EGG

1½ TEASPOONS ALMOND EXTRACT

1 TEASPOON VANILLA EXTRACT

½ TEASPOON RED FOOD COLORING

1. Preheat the oven to 350°.

2. In a small bowl, combine the flour and salt. In a large bowl, cream the butter and powdered sugar until light and fluffy. Add the egg, almond extract, and vanilla extract, and beat until smooth. Add the dry ingredients and stir until combined.

3. Divide the dough into halves. Mix half of the dough with the red food coloring until evenly colored.

4. For each cookie, shape 1 teaspoon of the plain dough into a 4-inch cylinder and then do the same for 1 teaspoon of the red dough. Place the 2 cylinders side-by-side; press together lightly and twist a few times.

5. Place the cookies on a baking sheet and curve 1 end to form a candy cane shape. Bake for 8 to 10 minutes, or until set and very lightly browned.

Variation: *Peppermint extract may be substituted for the almond extract. Or, tint some of the dough green instead of red and twist it together with plain dough for 2 varieties of "candy canes" to hang on your tree (and eat!).*

CHRISTMAS WREATHS

MAKES 6 DOZEN

3 STICKS BUTTER, AT ROOM
    TEMPERATURE
1 CUP PLUS 2 TABLESPOONS SUGAR
2 EGGS PLUS 1 EGG WHITE

2 TEASPOONS GRATED ORANGE ZEST
4 CUPS FLOUR
¼ CUP RED CANDIED CHERRIES
¼ CUP GREEN CANDIED CITRON

1. Preheat the oven to 350°.

2. In a large bowl, cream the butter and 1 cup of sugar until light and fluffy. Beat in the 2 eggs, 1 at a time, until incorporated. Stir in the orange zest. Stir in the flour until well blended.

3. Shape the dough by rounded teaspoonfuls into ropes about 6 inches long. Form each rope into a circle, crossing the ends and tucking them under. Place the cookies on a baking sheet.

4. In a medium bowl, beat the egg white and the remaining 2 tablespoons sugar until foamy. Brush the mixture over the tops of the cookies. Cut the candied cherries into small pieces to represent holly berries. Cut the citron into jagged shapes to represent leaves. Press a few pieces of candied cherries and citron on the part of the circles where the ends cross.

5. Bake for 10 to 12 minutes, or until set but not brown. Immediately remove the wreaths from the baking sheet.

Snickerdoodles

MAKES 5 DOZEN

2½ CUPS FLOUR

1 TEASPOON BAKING SODA

1 TEASPOON CREAM OF TARTAR

2 TEASPOONS CINNAMON

½ TEASPOON NUTMEG

¼ TEASPOON SALT

2 STICKS BUTTER, AT ROOM
  TEMPERATURE

1½ CUPS SUGAR

2 EGGS

1 TEASPOON VANILLA EXTRACT

1 CUP RAISINS

1 CUP COARSELY CHOPPED WALNUTS

1. Preheat the oven to 375°. Lightly grease a baking sheet.

2. In a small bowl, stir together the flour, baking soda, cream of tartar, 1 teaspoon of the cinnamon, the nutmeg, and salt.

3. In a large bowl, cream the butter and 1¼ cups of the sugar until light and fluffy. Beat in the eggs, 1 at a time, beating well after each addition. Beat in the vanilla. Gradually add the dry ingredients, beating well after each addition. Stir in the raisins and walnuts.

4. In a shallow bowl, stir together the remaining ¼ cup sugar and 1 teaspoon cinnamon. Shape the dough into 1-inch balls, then roll them in the cinnamon sugar. Place the balls on the prepared baking sheet, 2 inches apart. Bake for 12 to 15 minutes, or until the cookies have spread and are lightly browned around the edges.

5. Cool the cookies on a rack.

Jam Thumbprints

MAKES 2 DOZEN

1 STICK BUTTER, AT ROOM
   TEMPERATURE
⅓ CUP SUGAR
1 EGG YOLK

1 TEASPOON VANILLA EXTRACT
1⅓ CUPS FLOUR
¼ CUP JAM, JELLY, OR MARMALADE
⅓ CUP SLIVERED ALMONDS

1. Preheat the oven to 350°. Lightly grease a baking sheet.

2. In a large bowl, cream the butter until smooth and light. Add the sugar and beat until light and fluffy, then beat in the egg yolk and vanilla. Gradually add the flour and mix until completely incorporated. The dough should be very firm.

3. Shape the dough into 1-inch balls and place them on the prepared baking sheet, about 2 inches apart. With your thumb, make a deep indentation in the center of each cookie. Bake for 7 to 9 minutes, or until firm.

4. Remove the baking sheet from the oven and fill the center of each cookie with about ½ teaspoon of jam, then sprinkle with the slivered almonds. Return the cookies to the oven and continue baking for 6 to 8 minutes, or until the cookies are light golden brown around the edges.

5. Let the cookies cool on the baking sheet for 2 to 3 minutes, then transfer them to a rack to cool completely.

PEPPARKAKOR

MAKES 6 DOZEN

3½ CUPS FLOUR
1½ TEASPOONS GROUND GINGER
1½ TEASPOONS CINNAMON
1 TEASPOON GROUND CLOVES
¼ TEASPOON CARDAMOM
1 STICK BUTTER, AT ROOM
    TEMPERATURE
¾ CUP SUGAR

1 EGG
¾ CUP MOLASSES
2 TEASPOONS GRATED ORANGE ZEST
1 CUP POWDERED SUGAR
¼ TEASPOON VANILLA EXTRACT
4 TEASPOONS WATER
COLORED SUGAR (OPTIONAL)

1. In small bowl, combine the flour, ginger, cinnamon, cloves, and cardamom.

2. In a large bowl, cream the butter and ¾ cup sugar until light and fluffy. Beat in the egg and then the molasses and orange zest. Gradually stir in the dry ingredients and mix until blended. Wrap the dough in plastic wrap and chill for at least 4 hours, or overnight.

3. Preheat the oven to 375°. Lightly grease 2 baking sheets.

4. Roll out the dough on a lightly floured surface to ¼ inch thick. Cut into shapes with floured cookie cutters and place on the prepared baking sheets. Bake the cookies for 10 minutes, or until the edges start to brown. Cool on racks.

5. In a small bowl, combine the powdered sugar, vanilla, and water and stir until the frosting is smooth.

6. Frost the cooled cookies and sprinkle with colored sugar, if desired.

KITCHEN NOTE: *These Swedish iced spice cookies are similar to other European Christmas favorites. Germans bake pfeffernüsse, Danes enjoy pebernødder, and the Dutch feast on pepernoten.*

Hazelnut Macaroons

MAKES 20

1½ CUPS GROUND HAZELNUTS

6 TABLESPOONS COCOA POWDER

2 TABLESPOONS FINELY GRATED LEMON
   ZEST

PINCH OF SALT

1 TEASPOON VANILLA EXTRACT

2 EGG WHITES

¾ CUP SUGAR

1. Preheat the oven to 300°. Generously grease 2 large baking sheets.

2. In a small bowl, combine the hazelnuts, cocoa, lemon zest, salt, and vanilla; set aside.

3. In a large bowl, beat the egg whites until they foam and thicken slightly. Sprinkle the sugar over them and continue to beat until stiff peaks form. Gently but thoroughly fold the hazelnut mixture into the whites.

4. Drop the dough by tablespoonfuls onto the prepared baking sheets, 1 inch apart. Let the cookies rest at room temperature for 1 hour before baking.

5. Bake the cookies for 30 minutes, or until they are firm. Carefully transfer the cookies to a rack to cool.

SPRINGERLE

2 TABLESPOONS BUTTER, AT ROOM
  TEMPERATURE
1 CUP ANISE SEEDS
2 EGGS
1¼ CUPS SUGAR

1 TEASPOON FINELY GRATED LEMON
  ZEST
DROP OF VANILLA EXTRACT
3 CUPS FLOUR

1. With a pastry brush or paper towel, coat 2 large baking sheets with a tablespoon of butter each. Sprinkle the butter evenly with the anise seeds and set the pans aside.

2. In a large bowl, beat the eggs until they are thick and lemon-colored. Gradually add the sugar and continue beating until the mixture is thick enough to fall back on itself in a slowly dissolving ribbon when the beater is lifted from the bowl. Beat in the lemon zest and vanilla. Gradually add the flour, 1 cup at a time, until the dough is smooth.

3. Shape the dough into a ball and place it on a lightly floured surface. If the dough feels sticky, work additional flour into it with your fingers, adding a tablespoon at a time. Knead the dough with lightly floured hands for 10 minutes or so, until it is smooth and pliable.

4. Sprinkle the surface with flour again, pinch off about half of the dough, and roll it out into a rectangle about ¼ inch thick. Sprinkle a Springerle mold or Springerle rolling pin evenly with 2 tablespoons of flour, and rap it sharply on a table to remove the excess. Then press the mold down or roll the pin firmly across the dough, to print the pattern on it as deeply and clearly as possible. Cut the cookie squares apart with a small, sharp knife and place them 1 inch apart on the prepared baking sheets, pressing them gently into the anise seeds. Repeat the process with the rest of the dough. (You must work quickly because the dough dries rapidly.) Set the cookies aside uncovered at room temperature for 1 hour.

5. Preheat the oven to 250°.

6. Bake the cookies for 20 to 30 minutes, or until they are firm but not brown. Transfer the cookies to a rack to cool.

KITCHEN NOTE: *Wooden molds pressed into the dough emboss these German cookies with images of Saint Nicholas and the like. Springerle rolling pins have rows of images carved into them.*

ALMOND-PECAN SHORTBREAD

MAKES 40

2 STICKS BUTTER, AT ROOM
    TEMPERATURE
⅓ CUP LIGHT BROWN SUGAR
2 CUPS FLOUR

1 CUP CHOPPED ALMONDS
½ CUP CHOPPED PECANS
¼ TEASPOON ALMOND EXTRACT

1. In a large bowl, cream the butter and sugar, beating until fluffy. Gradually beat in the flour and blend well. Stir in the almonds, pecans, and almond extract. Shape the dough into a ball and then flatten it a bit. Wrap it in plastic wrap and refrigerate about an hour, or until firm.

2. Preheat the oven to 325°.

3. On a lightly floured surface, roll the dough into a 10 x 12½-inch rectangle about ¼ inch thick. Cut the dough into 2½-inch squares, then cut each square into 2 triangles.

4. Transfer the triangles to baking sheets and bake for 20 minutes, or until lightly browned. Cool the shortbread on racks.

KITCHEN NOTE: *Chilled dough is easier to handle, and you won't have to dust it with much flour to keep it from sticking. This trick can be used with any rolled or molded cookie.*

Pecan Lace Cookies

MAKES 8 DOZEN

1 STICK BUTTER, CUT INTO PIECES
⅔ CUP LIGHT BROWN SUGAR
½ CUP LIGHT CORN SYRUP
1 CUP FLOUR

1 CUP FINELY CHOPPED PECANS
½ TEASPOON VANILLA EXTRACT
2 OUNCES SEMISWEET CHOCOLATE
1 TEASPOON VEGETABLE SHORTENING

1. Preheat the oven to 375°. Lightly grease a baking sheet.

2. In a medium saucepan, warm the butter with the sugar and corn syrup over medium heat until the butter is melted and the mixture comes to a boil. Remove the pan from the heat, add the flour, pecans, and vanilla, and stir until combined.

3. Using a teaspoonful of batter for each cookie, drop the batter onto the prepared baking sheet, 3 inches apart (bake not more than 9 at a time). Bake for 5 to 7 minutes, or until the cookies spread to about 2½ inches and the surface looks caramelized and lacy.

4. Let the cookies cool on the baking sheet for 20 to 30 seconds. Transfer to a rack to cool completely. Let the baking sheet cool before making a second batch of cookies.

5. Meanwhile, in the top of a double boiler over hot, not simmering, water, melt the chocolate with the shortening and stir until smooth; transfer the glaze to a bowl.

6. With a spoon, drizzle the chocolate glaze over the cookies, or carefully half-dip the cookies into the glaze.

Gingersnaps

MAKES 4 DOZEN

2 CUPS FLOUR

2 TEASPOONS GROUND GINGER

1 TEASPOON BAKING SODA

¼ TEASPOON SALT

⅓ CUP BUTTER, AT ROOM
TEMPERATURE

⅓ CUP VEGETABLE SHORTENING

1 CUP DARK BROWN SUGAR

1 EGG

¼ CUP MOLASSES

2 TABLESPOONS GRANULATED SUGAR
(OPTIONAL)

1. Preheat the oven to 350°. Lightly grease a baking sheet.

2. In a small bowl, stir together the flour, ginger, baking soda, and salt.

3. In a large bowl, cream the butter, shortening, and brown sugar. Add the egg, and beat until light and fluffy, about 3 minutes. Beat in the molasses. Gradually add the dry ingredients, beating well until the dough is smooth.

4. Shape the dough into 1-inch balls and place them on the prepared baking sheet, 2 inches apart. Flatten the cookies to a ¼-inch thickness by pressing them with the bottom of a glass dipped in cold water. Bake for 9 to 11 minutes, or until the cookies are slightly puffed.

5. Transfer the cookies to a rack and, if desired, sprinkle them with the granulated sugar while still warm.

Spritz Cookies

2 CUPS FLOUR

½ TEASPOON BAKING POWDER

2 STICKS BUTTER, AT ROOM
   TEMPERATURE

⅓ CUP SUGAR

1 EGG

½ TEASPOON VANILLA EXTRACT

3 OUNCES SEMISWEET CHOCOLATE

4 TEASPOONS VEGETABLE SHORTENING

⅓ CUP FINELY CHOPPED ALMONDS

1. Preheat the oven to 350°. Lightly grease a baking sheet.

2. In a small bowl, stir together the flour and baking powder. In a large bowl, cream the butter and sugar until light and fluffy. Beat in the egg and vanilla. Gradually beat in the dry ingredients, beating well after each addition until the dough is smooth.

3. Fill a cookie press with the dough and form the cookies on the prepared baking sheet, 1 inch apart. Bake for 11 to 13 minutes, or until the edges are just beginning to turn golden.

4. Let the cookies cool on the baking sheet for 2 to 3 minutes, then transfer them to a rack to cool completely.

5. Meanwhile, in the top of a double boiler set over hot, not simmering, water, melt the chocolate with the shortening and stir until smooth.

6. Place the chopped almonds in a small bowl. Dip the cookies halfway into the chocolate glaze, then into the chopped almonds. Return the cookies to the rack until the glaze is set.

KITCHEN NOTE: *The word "spritz" means "squirt" in German— which is descriptive of how dough comes out of a cookie press. The press consists of a wide cylinder fitted with interchangeable plates that turn out cookies in various shapes.*

PFEFFERNÜSSE

MAKES 30

4 CUPS FLOUR

1 TEASPOON BAKING POWDER

1 TEASPOON GROUND CLOVES

½ TEASPOON ALLSPICE

½ TEASPOON CINNAMON

¾ CUP HONEY

1 CUP DARK CORN SYRUP

¾ CUP SUGAR

2 TABLESPOONS BUTTER

1 TABLESPOON VEGETABLE SHORTENING

1. Preheat the oven to 400°. Lightly grease 2 large baking sheets.

2. In a small bowl, combine the flour, baking powder, cloves, allspice, and cinnamon; set aside.

3. In a large saucepan, bring the honey, corn syrup, and sugar to a boil over medium heat, stirring until the sugar dissolves. Reduce the heat to low and simmer, uncovered, for 5 minutes. Remove the pan from the heat, add the butter and shortening, and stir until melted. Beat in the dry ingredients, 1 cup at a time, beating well after each addition.

4. Drop the dough by teaspoonfuls onto the baking sheets, about 1 inch apart. Bake for about 15 minutes, or until the cookies are firm to the touch and light brown. Transfer them to a rack to cool and proceed with the remaining batches, greasing the baking sheets again as needed.

KITCHEN NOTE: *If you're the plan-ahead type, these are the holiday cookies for you: They're best when made in advance and stored in a tightly covered tin or jar. After a week, their flavor will mellow and their texture will improve. Anise lovers may want to add ¼ teaspoon of the crushed seeds to the dry ingredients.*

Soft Molasses Cookies

MAKES 4 DOZEN

2½ TO 3 CUPS FLOUR
1 TABLESPOON BAKING SODA
2 TEASPOONS CINNAMON
2 TEASPOONS GROUND GINGER
¼ TEASPOON SALT

¾ CUP VEGETABLE SHORTENING
¾ CUP SUGAR
¾ CUP DARK MOLASSES
¾ CUP SOUR CREAM
2 EGGS, LIGHTLY BEATEN

1. Preheat the oven to 350°. Lightly grease 2 large baking sheets.

2. In a medium bowl, combine 2 cups of the flour, the baking soda, cinnamon, ginger, and salt.

3. In a large bowl, cream the shortening and sugar until light and fluffy. Beat in the molasses until well incorporated. Add the sour cream and the eggs and beat until smooth. Stir in the dry ingredients, ½ cup at a time, beating well after each addition.

4. Spread ½ cup of flour on a plate. Flour your hands to prevent the dough from sticking. To make each cookie, break off a heaping teaspoon of the dough, coat it with the flour on the plate, and with your hands, roll it into a ball about 1 inch in diameter. Sprinkle more flour on the plate if necessary. As you shape the cookie balls, arrange them, 2 inches apart, on the prepared baking sheets.

5. Bake for 8 to 10 minutes, or until the cookies feel firm when prodded gently with a finger. Transfer the cookies to racks to cool.

Rugelach

MAKES 32

2 STICKS UNSALTED BUTTER, AT ROOM
  TEMPERATURE
8 OUNCES CREAM CHEESE, AT ROOM
  TEMPERATURE
2 CUPS FLOUR

½ CUP SUGAR
1 TEASPOON CINNAMON
½ CUP RAISINS
¾ CUP FINELY CHOPPED WALNUTS

1. In a large bowl, cream the butter and the cream cheese until light and fluffy. Beat in the flour, ½ cup at a time, and continue to beat until the dough is smooth and can be gathered into a ball. Divide the dough into 2 portions, wrap in plastic wrap, and refrigerate for at least 1 hour, or until firm.

2. Meanwhile, in a large bowl, combine the sugar, cinnamon, raisins, and walnuts; set the filling aside.

3. Preheat the oven to 350°.

4. Place 1 portion of the dough between 2 sheets of wax paper and roll it out to a circle about 10 inches in diameter. Peel off the top sheet and, using a 9-inch cake pan as a guide, cut out a 9-inch circle of dough.

5. Start at the center of the circle and, with a small knife or pastry wheel, cut the dough as you would a pie, into 16 narrow wedges. Sprinkle the filling evenly over the dough, and cover with another sheet of wax paper. With a rolling pin, press down on the wax paper so that the filling adheres to the dough. Peel off the top sheet of wax paper and, starting with the large end, roll up each triangle. Tuck under the pointed end of each cookie and place on a baking sheet, 2 inches apart. Repeat the process with the remaining dough.

6. Bake for 15 to 18 minutes, until light golden, then transfer to racks to cool.

KITCHEN NOTE: *These eastern European cookies are like miniature crescent pastries; they're made with a rich cream-cheese dough and filled with dried fruit and nuts. Sometimes jam or chocolate is incorporated into the filling.*

LICORICE COOKIES

MAKES 5 DOZEN

2½ CUPS FLOUR
½ TEASPOON SALT
2 STICKS BUTTER, AT ROOM
  TEMPERATURE

¾ CUP SUGAR
1 EGG PLUS 1 EGG YOLK
1 TABLESPOON ANISE SEEDS
½ TEASPOON ANISE EXTRACT

1. In a small bowl, stir together the flour and salt; set aside.

2. In a large bowl, cream the butter and the sugar until light and fluffy. Beat in the egg and egg yolk, then add the anise seeds and anise extract. Beat in the flour mixture about ½ cup at a time. If the dough becomes too stiff to stir easily, incorporate the remaining flour with your hands.

3. Pat and shape the dough into 2 cylinders, each about 1½ inches in diameter. Wrap the cylinders in wax paper and refrigerate for at least 1 hour.

4. Preheat the oven to 350°. Lightly grease 2 large baking sheets.

5. Slice 1 cylinder of dough crosswise into ¼-inch-thick rounds. For each cookie, roll a slice between your palms until it forms a rope about 4 inches long and ¼ inch in diameter. Drape the rope into a loop on the prepared baking sheet and cross the ends so that the loop looks like a handwritten letter "l." Arrange the cookies 1 inch apart. Bake for 10 to 12 minutes, or until the cookies are delicately browned. Transfer the cookies to racks to cool.

Oatmeal Scotchies

MAKES 2 DOZEN

1½ CUPS FLOUR
1 TEASPOON BAKING SODA
½ TEASPOON SALT
2 STICKS BUTTER, AT ROOM
   TEMPERATURE
¼ CUP VEGETABLE OIL
¾ CUP DARK BROWN SUGAR

⅓ CUP GRANULATED SUGAR
1 EGG
1 TEASPOON VANILLA EXTRACT
3 CUPS ROLLED OATS
ONE 6-OUNCE PACKAGE
   BUTTERSCOTCH CHIPS
1 CUP COARSELY CHOPPED PECANS

1. Preheat the oven to 375°. Lightly grease a baking sheet.

2. In a small bowl, stir together the flour, baking soda, and salt.

3. In a large bowl, cream the butter, vegetable oil, and sugars until light and fluffy. Beat in the egg and vanilla. Gradually add the dry ingredients, stirring just until incorporated. Stir in the oats, butterscotch chips, and pecans.

4. Drop ¼-cup portions of the cookie dough onto the prepared baking sheet, 3 to 4 inches apart. Flatten each portion of dough slightly with your fingertips. Bake for 13 to 15 minutes, or until the cookies are lightly browned on the edges.

5. Let the cookies cool on the baking sheet for 2 to 3 minutes, then transfer them to a rack to cool completely.

CHOCOLATE PRETZELS

MAKES 25

1 STICK UNSALTED BUTTER, AT ROOM
   TEMPERATURE
¼ CUP PLUS ⅔ CUP SUGAR
¼ CUP COCOA POWDER
3 TABLESPOONS HOT WATER
2 CUPS FLOUR
1 EGG, LIGHTLY BEATEN

1 TEASPOON VANILLA EXTRACT
½ CUP MILK
2 OUNCES SEMISWEET CHOCOLATE
2 OUNCES UNSWEETENED CHOCOLATE
½ CUP LIGHT CORN SYRUP
1 TEASPOON BUTTER

1. In a large bowl, cream the unsalted butter and ¼ cup of sugar until light and fluffy. Dissolve the cocoa in the hot water and let it cool to room temperature. Beat it into the butter-sugar mixture. Beat in the flour, 1 cup at a time, until incorporated. Add the egg and vanilla and beat until smooth. Pat and shape the dough into a cylinder about 7 inches long and 2 inches in diameter. Wrap in wax paper and refrigerate for 30 minutes, or until firm.

2. Preheat the oven to 350°.

3. Slice the dough crosswise into about 25 equal pieces and roll each slice between your hands to make a ropelike strip about 14 inches long and ¼ inch in diameter. Form each rope into a pretzel shape. Arrange the pretzels 1 inch apart on baking sheets and bake for 10 minutes, or until they are firm to the touch. Transfer the pretzels to a rack to cool.

4. Meanwhile, combine the milk, ⅔ cup of sugar, semisweet chocolate, unsweetened chocolate, and corn syrup in the top of a double boiler. Cook over simmering water, stirring constantly, until the sugar is dissolved and the chocolate is melted. Stir in 1 teaspoon of butter, remove the pan from the heat, and cool to lukewarm.

5. With tongs, dip the pretzels into the glaze 1 at a time to coat them thoroughly. Dry them for at least 15 minutes on a rack set over wax paper.

Honey Cookies

MAKES 2 DOZEN

1 STICK UNSALTED BUTTER, MELTED
¼ CUP HONEY
¼ CUP SUGAR
1 TEASPOON BAKING SODA
1 EGG YOLK

1 CUP FLOUR
½ CUP COARSE WHITE DECORATING
   SUGAR

1. Preheat the oven to 350°.

2. In a large bowl, combine the butter, honey, sugar, baking soda, and egg yolk, and beat vigorously with a wooden spoon until the ingredients are thoroughly mixed. Gradually sift in the flour, a few tablespoons at a time, beating well after each addition. The dough should be just firm enough to be gathered into a soft but compact ball.

3. To shape each cookie, pinch off about 1 rounded teaspoon of dough and, on a heavily floured surface, roll it with the palm of your hand into a ball. Dip the top of the ball into the coarse sugar and place it sugared-side up on a baking sheet. Make similar balls of the remaining dough and arrange them ½ inch apart on the baking sheet. Bake for 10 minutes, or until delicately browned. Transfer the cookies to a rack to cool.

BLACK-AND-WHITE PINWHEEL COOKIES

MAKES 8 DOZEN

2 STICKS BUTTER, AT ROOM
TEMPERATURE
1 CUP SUGAR
1 EGG PLUS 1 EGG YOLK

1 TEASPOON VANILLA EXTRACT
2¼ CUPS FLOUR
2 TABLESPOONS COCOA POWDER

1. In a large bowl, cream the butter and sugar until light and fluffy. Beat in the egg and egg yolk, then beat in the vanilla. Gradually add the flour, beating just until incorporated.

2. Divide the dough into 2 equal portions. Thoroughly mix the cocoa into 1 portion. Form each portion of dough into a ball.

3. Divide each ball of dough into 4 equal portions, then roll each out to a 6 x 5-inch rectangle. Place a dark rectangle on top of a light one and roll the 2 sheets together tightly from 1 long side, like a jelly roll. Wrap each roll in plastic wrap and refrigerate for at least 4 hours.

4. Preheat the oven to 350°. Lightly grease a baking sheet.

5. Use a sharp knife to cut the dough into ¼-inch-thick slices. Place the cookies on the prepared baking sheet, 1 inch apart, and bake for 8 to 10 minutes, or until lightly browned around the edges. Cool the cookies on a rack.

VARIATION: *For bull's-eye cookies, divide each ball of dough into 4 portions as directed. Roll the portions of chocolate dough out into 4 x 6-inch rectangles and form the vanilla dough into 6-inch-long logs. Wrap each vanilla log in a sheet of chocolate dough; smooth the seam. Wrap, chill, cut, and bake the cookies as directed above.*

Cinnamon-Walnut Cookies

MAKES 8 DOZEN

3½ CUPS FLOUR

2 TEASPOONS BAKING POWDER

1 TEASPOON SALT

2 STICKS BUTTER, AT ROOM
TEMPERATURE

2⅓ CUPS SUGAR

3 EGGS

1 TEASPOON VANILLA EXTRACT

2 TEASPOONS CINNAMON

1 CUP FINELY CHOPPED WALNUTS

½ CUP MILK

1. In a medium bowl, combine the flour, baking powder, and salt, and sift them together onto a plate or a sheet of wax paper.

2. In a large bowl, cream the butter and 2 cups of the sugar until light and fluffy. Beat in the eggs, 1 at a time, beating well after each addition. Beat in the flour mixture, 1 cup at a time, until incorporated. Add the vanilla and continue to beat until the dough is smooth. Cover the dough with plastic wrap and refrigerate for at least 8 hours, or overnight.

3. Preheat the oven to 350°. Grease 2 large baking sheets.

4. In a small bowl, combine the remaining ⅓ cup of sugar, the cinnamon, and walnuts; set aside.

5. Cut off about ¼ of the dough and shape it into a ball. Return the rest of the dough to the refrigerator. On a lightly floured surface, roll

the ball of dough out into a rough circle about ⅛ inch thick. With a floured cookie cutter, cut the dough into 2-inch rounds. Brush the tops of the cookies lightly with milk and sprinkle them with a little of the sugar-walnut mixture.

6. Place the cookies 1 inch apart on the prepared baking sheets. Bake for 8 to 10 minutes, or until the cookies are crisp around the edges and the tops feel firm when prodded gently with a finger. Transfer the cookies to racks to cool.

7. Let the baking sheets cool completely, then repeat the entire procedure 3 more times, greasing the pans again for each batch of cookies and rolling and baking ¼ of the dough at a time.

Linzer Tarts

MAKES 2 DOZEN

2 CUPS FLOUR
½ TEASPOON SALT
1½ STICKS BUTTER, AT ROOM
    TEMPERATURE

⅓ CUP SUGAR
2 EGGS
POWDERED SUGAR
½ CUP RASPBERRY JAM

1. In a small bowl, combine the flour and salt; set aside.

2. In a large bowl, cream the butter and sugar until light and fluffy. Beat in the eggs, 1 at a time, beating well after each addition. Gradually add the flour mixture and beat until smooth. Divide the dough into 2 portions, wrap in plastic wrap, and refrigerate at least 4 hours, or overnight.

3. Preheat the oven to 375°

4. On a lightly floured surface, roll 1 portion of the dough to ⅛ inch thick. Cut out the dough with a 3-inch round cookie cutter. Roll and cut out the other portion of dough with a 3-inch doughnut cutter. Bake the cookies for 8 to 10 minutes, or until set. Cool on a rack.

5. Sift powdered sugar over the doughnut-cut cookies. Spread jam on the rest of the cookies. Carefully sandwich the cookies together.

KITCHEN NOTE: *If you don't have a doughnut cutter, cut all the cookie rounds with the same cookie cutter and then use a makeshift implement to create the center hole. Scout your kitchen drawers and cabinets for something of the appropriate size: A widemouthed bottle, a small jar, or a small shot glass are possibilities.*

Pecan Balls

MAKES 3 DOZEN

1½ CUPS PECAN HALVES, FINELY
  CHOPPED
1 STICK BUTTER, AT ROOM
  TEMPERATURE

¼ CUP GRANULATED SUGAR
2 TEASPOONS VANILLA EXTRACT
2 CUPS FLOUR
¼ CUP POWDERED SUGAR

1. Preheat the oven to 300°. Lightly grease a baking sheet.

2. Place the pecans in a skillet. Toast them over medium-high heat, shaking the pan frequently, until golden brown, 5 to 8 minutes.

3. In a large bowl, cream the butter and granulated sugar until light and fluffy. Beat in the vanilla. Gradually add the flour, beating until just incorporated. Stir in the pecans. The dough will be firm and slightly crumbly.

4. Shape the dough into 1-inch balls and place them on the prepared baking sheet, 1 inch apart. Bake for 18 to 20 minutes, or until the cookies just begin to brown around the edges. The tops should remain pale.

5. Let the cookies cool on the baking sheet for 5 minutes, then carefully transfer them to a rack. While the cookies are still warm, sift the powdered sugar over them, then cool completely.

GIANT CHOCOLATE-
CHOCOLATE CHIP COOKIES

MAKES 1 DOZEN

ONE 6-OUNCE PACKAGE SEMISWEET
  CHOCOLATE CHIPS
2 TABLESPOONS MILK
1 CUP PLUS 2 TABLESPOONS FLOUR
2 TABLESPOONS COCOA POWDER
½ TEASPOON BAKING SODA

½ TEASPOON SALT
1 STICK BUTTER, AT ROOM
  TEMPERATURE
⅔ CUP BROWN SUGAR
1 EGG

1. Preheat the oven to 375°.

2. In a small saucepan, combine ⅓ cup of the chocolate chips and the milk and let sit over very low heat until the chocolate is melted, 5 to 10 minutes. Stir the chocolate mixture until smooth and blended. Remove the pan from the heat and set aside.

3. Meanwhile, in a medium bowl, stir together the flour, cocoa, baking soda, and salt.

4. In another medium bowl, cream the butter and sugar until light and fluffy. Beat in the

egg until well blended, then blend in the chocolate mixture. Beat in the flour mixture just until combined, then stir in the remaining chocolate chips.

5. Drop ¼-cup portions of dough onto a baking sheet, about 3 inches apart. Gently flatten the dough to form 2½-inch rounds.

6. Bake the cookies for 10 to 12 minutes, or until the bottoms are lightly browned. Undercook them somewhat if you prefer chewy cookies.

PECAn-STUFFED DATE COOKiES

MAKES 45

45 PITTED DATES
45 SHELLED PECAN HALVES
2 CUPS FLOUR
½ TEASPOON BAKING POWDER
½ TEASPOON BAKING SODA
½ TEASPOON SALT
1½ STICKS BUTTER, AT ROOM
   TEMPERATURE

¾ CUP LIGHT BROWN SUGAR
2 EGGS
½ CUP SOUR CREAM
1 TEASPOON PLUS 1 TABLESPOON
   VANILLA EXTRACT
3 CUPS POWDERED SUGAR
3 TO 4 TABLESPOONS MILK

1. Preheat the oven to 350°. Generously grease 2 large baking sheets. Gently pry each date open along the slit in its side, insert a pecan half, and press the edges of the date securely together. Set aside.

2. In a small bowl, combine the flour, baking powder, baking soda, and salt; set aside.

3. In a large bowl, cream ½ stick of butter and the brown sugar until light and fluffy. Beat in the eggs, 1 at a time, beating well after each addition. Alternating between the 2, beat in the flour mixture and the sour cream, beating well after each addition. Stir in 1 teaspoon of the vanilla extract.

4. With tongs, pick up 1 pecan-stuffed date at a time and swirl it in the batter to coat the entire surface evenly. As they are coated,

arrange the dates about 1 inch apart on the prepared baking sheets. Bake for 10 minutes, or until the coating is delicately browned. Then transfer the cookies to racks to cool to room temperature.

5. Meanwhile, melt the remaining stick of butter over low heat. Pour the melted butter into a mixing bowl and, when it has cooled, sift in the powdered sugar. Mix well, then stir in 1 tablespoon of vanilla extract and 3 tablespoons of milk. If the icing is too stiff to spread easily, add up to 1 tablespoon more milk, 1 teaspoon at a time.

6. Spread the icing evenly over the entire outside surface of each of the cookies and arrange them side by side on wax paper to dry.

Cinnamon Pinwheels

MAKES 2 DOZEN

2 STICKS BUTTER, AT ROOM
    TEMPERATURE
1½ CUPS FLOUR
½ CUP SOUR CREAM

6 TABLESPOONS SUGAR
1 TEASPOON CINNAMON
1 TABLESPOON WATER

1. In a large bowl, with a pastry blender or 2 knives, cut the butter into the flour until it resembles coarse crumbs. Stir in the sour cream until well combined. Cover the dough and refrigerate at least 8 hours, or overnight.

2. In a small bowl, combine 3 tablespoons of sugar with the cinnamon; set aside.

3. Sprinkle some sugar and flour over the work surface. Divide the dough into 2 equal portions. Roll 1 portion into a rectangle 20 x 7 inches. Sprinkle the dough with half of the sugar-cinnamon mixture. Beginning at a short side, roll the dough up tightly. Roll the other portion of dough into a rectangle 20 x 7

inches; sprinkle with the remaining sugar-cinnamon mixture. Attach the loose end of the roll to the new rectangle; pinch the edges to seal. Continue to roll up tightly; pinch the ending edge of dough into the roll to seal. Wrap the roll in wax paper and refrigerate at least 1 hour, or until firm.

4. Preheat the oven to 350°.

5. Cut the roll into ¼-inch slices. Place the slices 2 inches apart on a baking sheet. In a small bowl, combine the remaining 3 tablespoons sugar with the water and brush the mixture over the cookies. Bake for 20 to 25 minutes, or until golden.

ALMOND MERINGUES

MAKES 2 DOZEN

1 EGG WHITE
1 CUP LIGHT BROWN SUGAR, SIFTED

1½ CUPS COARSELY CHOPPED ALMONDS

1. Preheat the oven to 250°. Grease 2 large baking sheets.

2. In a medium bowl, beat the egg white until stiff peaks form. Beat in the brown sugar, about ¼ cup at a time, and continue to beat until the meringue mixture is very stiff and no longer glossy. Gently fold in the almonds.

3. Scoop up about 1 tablespoonful of the mixture and, with the aid of another spoon, slide it in a small mound onto the prepared baking sheets. Arrange the meringues about 1 inch apart on the baking sheets. Bake for 30 minutes, or until the meringues have lost all their sheen and are a pale biscuit color. Transfer the meringues to a rack to cool.

Hermits

MAKES 4 DOZEN

2 CUPS FLOUR

1 TEASPOON CINNAMON

½ TEASPOON ALLSPICE

½ TEASPOON NUTMEG

½ TEASPOON BAKING POWDER

¼ TEASPOON SALT

1 STICK BUTTER, AT ROOM
    TEMPERATURE

¾ CUP DARK BROWN SUGAR

2 EGGS

¼ CUP MOLASSES

1 TEASPOON VANILLA EXTRACT

1 CUP GOLDEN RAISINS

1 CUP COARSELY CHOPPED ALMONDS

1. Preheat the oven to 350°. Lightly grease a baking sheet.

2. In a small bowl, stir together the flour, cinnamon, allspice, nutmeg, baking powder, and salt.

3. In a large bowl, cream the butter and sugar until light and fluffy. Beat in the eggs, 1 at a time, beating well after each addition. Beat in the molasses and the vanilla. Gradually add the flour mixture and continue beating until smooth. Stir in the raisins and the almonds.

4. Drop the cookie dough by tablespoonfuls onto the prepared baking sheet, 2 inches apart. Bake for 15 to 17 minutes, or until the cookies are lightly browned on the edges.

5. Cool the cookies on a rack.

KITCHEN NOTE: *Some say that these classic New England cookies got their name because they keep so well—a quality that makes them great for holiday giving. Pack the cookies in pairs, bottoms together, and fit them snugly in the box so they don't get shaken around and crumble in transit. An empty oatmeal box makes a gift box: Cover the box and lid with wrapping paper before filling it.*

Fruit Fold-Ups

MAKES 3 DOZEN

1½ CUPS FLOUR

½ CUP WHOLE-WHEAT FLOUR

2 TABLESPOONS GRANULATED SUGAR

1 TEASPOON BAKING POWDER

½ TEASPOON BAKING SODA

¼ TEASPOON SALT

1½ STICKS COLD BUTTER, CUT INTO
    PIECES

1 EGG, LIGHTLY BEATEN

1 TEASPOON VANILLA EXTRACT

4 CUPS MIXED DRIED FRUITS

1½ CUPS DARK BROWN SUGAR

⅔ CUP APPLE JUICE

3 TABLESPOONS HONEY

1. In a large bowl, combine the flours, granulated sugar, baking powder, baking soda, and salt. With a pastry blender or 2 knives, cut in the butter until the mixture resembles cornmeal. Add the egg and vanilla, and stir until smooth. Wrap the dough in plastic wrap and refrigerate until ready to use.

2. In a medium saucepan, combine the dried fruits, brown sugar, apple juice, and honey. Cook over medium heat, stirring occasionally, until the mixture comes to a boil. Cover the pan, reduce the heat, and simmer the mixture for 10 to 15 minutes, or until the fruits are softened. Set aside to cool completely.

3. In a food processor or blender, process the fruit mixture until uniformly chopped but not completely smooth. Transfer the filling to a bowl, cover it with plastic wrap, and refrigerate for at least 30 minutes, or until firm.

4. Preheat the oven to 375°.

5. Divide the dough into 2 equal portions. On a lightly floured surface, roll out each portion of dough to a 15 x 6½-inch rectangle. Spoon a 3-inch-wide strip of filling down the center of each rectangle of dough, leaving a ½-inch border at each end.

6. Fold both sides of the dough lengthwise over the filling, and press the edges lightly to seal them. Turn the filled loaves seam-side down, then press them gently to flatten them to a width of about 3 inches. Transfer the loaves to a baking sheet, leaving at least an inch of space between them, and bake for 20 to 25 minutes, or until golden brown.

7. Let cool on the baking sheet for 15 minutes, then transfer to a rack to cool completely. Cut into ¾-inch-wide slices.

FIG SQUARES

MAKES 4 DOZEN

¾ CUP FLOUR

1 TEASPOON BAKING POWDER

¼ TEASPOON GROUND CLOVES

¼ TEASPOON CINNAMON

¼ TEASPOON SALT

3 EGGS

1 CUP SUGAR

1 TEASPOON VANILLA EXTRACT

2 CUPS FINELY CHOPPED DRIED FIGS

1 CUP FINELY CHOPPED WALNUTS

POWDERED SUGAR

1. Preheat the oven to 325°. Grease and flour the bottom and sides of a 13 x 9 x 2-inch baking pan.

2. In a small bowl, combine the flour, baking powder, cloves, cinnamon, and salt; set aside.

3. In a large bowl, beat the eggs until they are smooth. Alternately add the flour mixture and the sugar, beating well after each addition. Stir in the vanilla, figs, and walnuts.

4. Pour the batter into the prepared pan and smooth the top with a spatula. Bake for 25 minutes, or until the top is delicately browned and firm to the touch. Place on a rack to cool to room temperature. Cut into individual 1½-inch squares. Sift a little powdered sugar evenly over the squares.

KITCHEN NOTE: *Figs and other sticky dried fruits are easier to chop if you first chill them in the freezer for an hour. Spraying the knife blade with nonstick cooking spray also speeds the process.*

Apricot-Nut Bars

1½ CUPS DRIED APRICOTS
½ CUP APPLE JUICE
¼ CUP LIGHT BROWN SUGAR
1½ CUPS FLOUR
½ TEASPOON BAKING SODA
¼ TEASPOON SALT

1 STICK COLD BUTTER, CUT INTO
    PIECES
1 CUP CHOPPED WALNUTS
⅓ CUP GRANULATED SUGAR
2 TEASPOONS GRATED ORANGE ZEST

1. Preheat the oven to 350°. Grease and flour an 8-inch square baking pan.

2. In a small saucepan, combine the apricots, apple juice, and brown sugar, and bring to a boil over medium heat. Cover the pan, reduce the heat to medium-low, and simmer the mixture until the apricots are tender, about 10 minutes. Remove the pan from the heat and set aside, uncovered, to cool slightly.

3. Transfer the apricot mixture to a food processor or blender and process, pulsing the machine on and off, until the mixture is a spreadable consistency, 5 to 10 seconds. Set the filling aside.

4. In a medium bowl, stir together the flour, baking soda, and salt. With a pastry blender or 2 knives, cut in the butter until the mixture resembles cornmeal. Stir in the walnuts, granulated sugar, and orange zest; the mixture will be crumbly. Set aside ⅔ cup of the crust mixture for the topping, then pat the remaining mixture evenly on the bottom of the prepared baking pan. Bake the crust for 10 minutes, or until firm.

5. Carefully spread the apricot filling over the crust, then sprinkle the reserved crust mixture evenly over the filling. Bake for another 25 to 30 minutes, or until the topping is golden.

6. Let cool in the pan on a rack, then cut into 20 bars.

CHOCOLATE-TOFFEE BARS

MAKES 20

2 STICKS PLUS 4 TABLESPOONS BUTTER,
   AT ROOM TEMPERATURE
1 CUP GRANULATED SUGAR
1 EGG
2 CUPS FLOUR

1 CUP WHOLE ALMONDS
⅔ CUP DARK BROWN SUGAR
1½ TEASPOONS VANILLA EXTRACT
2 OUNCES SEMISWEET CHOCOLATE
1 TABLESPOON VEGETABLE SHORTENING

1. Preheat the oven to 300°. Grease and flour an 11 x 7-inch baking pan.

2. In a medium bowl, cream 2 sticks of the butter and the granulated sugar. Beat in the egg, then add the flour and mix until blended. Spread the dough evenly in the bottom of the prepared pan and bake for 20 minutes. Set the crust aside to cool slightly. Increase the oven temperature to 350°.

3. Meanwhile, place the almonds in a skillet and toast them over medium-high heat, shaking the pan frequently, until golden brown, 5 to 10 minutes. Briefly cool, then coarsely chop the almonds.

4. In a small saucepan, combine the remaining 4 tablespoons of butter with the brown sugar and cook over medium heat until the butter is melted and the sugar is dissolved. Remove the pan from the heat and stir in 1 teaspoon of the vanilla.

5. Spread the sugar mixture evenly over the crust. Sprinkle the chopped almonds on top and bake for another 20 minutes, or until the topping is set.

6. Meanwhile, in the top of a double boiler over hot, not simmering, water, melt the chocolate and shortening, stirring until smooth. Stir in the remaining ½ teaspoon of vanilla.

7. Drizzle the chocolate glaze over the nut topping. Let cool in the pan on a rack, then cut into 20 bars.

Peanut Butter-Chocolate Chip Brownies

MAKES 16

1½ CUPS FLOUR

¾ TEASPOON BAKING POWDER

¼ TEASPOON SALT

1 STICK BUTTER

½ CUP CHUNKY PEANUT BUTTER

1 CUP SUGAR

2 EGGS

1 TEASPOON VANILLA EXTRACT

1 CUP CHOCOLATE CHIPS

1. Preheat the oven to 375°. Grease and flour an 8-inch square baking pan.

2. In a small bowl, combine the flour, baking powder, and salt; set aside.

3. In a large bowl, cream the butter and peanut butter. Beat in the sugar. Beat in the eggs, 1 at a time, then beat in the vanilla. Gradually add the flour mixture, beating until just incorporated. Stir in the chocolate chips.

4. Spread the batter in the prepared baking pan and bake for 35 minutes, or until golden brown on top and a toothpick inserted in the center comes out clean.

5. Let cool in the pan on a rack before cutting into 16 squares.

Substitution: *Fans of this flavor combination will be ecstatic if you substitute 6 ounces of coarsely chopped peanut-butter cups for the chocolate chips. Chilling the candy will make it easier to chop.*

DREAM BARS

MAKES 20

1 CUP PLUS 2 TABLESPOONS FLOUR

1 CUP DARK BROWN SUGAR

1 STICK COLD BUTTER, CUT INTO
PIECES

1 CUP SHREDDED COCONUT

1 CUP COARSELY CHOPPED PECANS

¾ TEASPOON BAKING POWDER

¼ TEASPOON SALT

2 EGGS

1 TEASPOON VANILLA EXTRACT

1 TEASPOON GRATED LEMON ZEST

1. Preheat the oven to 375°. Grease and flour an 11 x 7-inch baking pan.

2. In a medium bowl, stir together 1 cup of the flour and ¼ cup of the brown sugar. With a fork, mix in the butter until the mixture resembles very coarse crumbs. Press the mixture into the prepared baking pan and bake for 10 minutes.

3. Meanwhile, in a small bowl, combine the coconut, pecans, baking powder, salt, and the remaining 2 tablespoons flour.

4. In a medium bowl, beat together the eggs, vanilla, lemon zest, and the remaining ¾ cup

brown sugar. Add the flour mixture and stir until combined.

5. Remove the pan from the oven and let the crust cool slightly. Pour the coconut-pecan mixture over the crust, spreading it evenly with a spatula, and bake for another 18 to 20 minutes, or until the topping is golden brown and set.

6. Let cool slightly in the pan on a rack, then cut into 20 bars while still warm.

Lemon Squares
with Jam Filling

MAKES 15

2 CUPS PLUS 3 TABLESPOONS FLOUR

⅓ CUP POWDERED SUGAR, PLUS EXTRA
    FOR DUSTING

¼ TEASPOON SALT

2 STICKS COLD BUTTER, CUT INTO
    PIECES

1¼ CUPS GRANULATED SUGAR

½ TEASPOON BAKING POWDER

3 EGGS

⅓ CUP FRESH LEMON JUICE

2 TEASPOONS GRATED LEMON ZEST

¾ CUP STRAWBERRY OR RASPBERRY JAM

1. Preheat the oven to 350°. Grease and flour an 11 x 7-inch baking pan.

2. In a large bowl, stir together 2 cups of the flour, ⅓ cup of the powdered sugar, and the salt. With a pastry blender or 2 knives, cut in the butter until the mixture resembles coarse crumbs. Press the mixture into the prepared baking pan and bake for 15 minutes, or just until firm.

3. Meanwhile, in a medium bowl, stir together the granulated sugar, baking powder, and the remaining 3 tablespoons flour. Add the eggs, lemon juice, and lemon zest, and mix until well blended.

4. Remove the pan from the oven and spread the jam over the crust. Spread the lemon mixture over the jam and bake for another 25 to 30 minutes, or until the topping is set.

5. Let cool in the pan on a rack. Dust the top lightly with powdered sugar before cutting into 15 squares.

APPLE BARS

MAKES 20

6 MEDIUM GRANNY SMITH OR OTHER
  TART APPLES
2 TABLESPOONS FRESH LEMON JUICE
4 CUPS FLOUR
1 TEASPOON BAKING POWDER
½ TEASPOON BAKING SODA

1¼ CUPS SUGAR
½ CUP VEGETABLE OIL
2 EGGS
1½ TEASPOONS VANILLA EXTRACT
1 TABLESPOON CINNAMON

1. Preheat the oven to 350°. Grease and flour a 13 x 9-inch baking pan.

2. Peel and coarsely grate the apples. Place them in a large bowl and toss them with the lemon juice, then set aside in a colander to drain.

3. In a medium bowl, stir together the flour, baking powder, and baking soda.

4. In a large bowl, beat together ¾ cup of the sugar and the oil. Beat in the eggs, 1 at a time, beating well after each addition. Beat in the vanilla. Gradually add the flour mixture, stirring until well combined. The dough should be very stiff; add a little more flour if it does not seem stiff enough to grate.

5. Divide the dough into 2 equal portions. Press half of the dough evenly into the bottom of the prepared pan. Pat the grated apples dry with paper towels, then spread them evenly over the bottom layer of dough.

6. In a small bowl, stir together the remaining sugar and the cinnamon. Sprinkle the apples with half of the cinnamon sugar.

7. Using the coarse side of a grater, grate the remaining dough over the apples, covering them as completely as possible; do not press or flatten the dough. Sprinkle the remaining cinnamon sugar over the topping and bake for 55 to 60 minutes, or until the topping is crisp and golden.

8. Let cool in the pan on a rack, then cut into 20 large bars. Serve warm. If not serving immediately, reheat briefly before serving to crisp the topping.

CHOCOLATE-APRICOT BARS

MAKES 32

⅓ CUP BUTTER

ONE 9-OUNCE PACKAGE CHOCOLATE
  WAFERS

½ TEASPOON VANILLA EXTRACT

ONE 14-OUNCE CAN SWEETENED
  CONDENSED MILK

1 CUP DRIED APRICOTS, COARSELY
  CHOPPED

1 CUP CHOPPED PECANS

ONE 6-OUNCE PACKAGE SEMISWEET
  CHOCOLATE CHIPS

1. Preheat the oven to 350°.

2. Melt the butter in a small saucepan or in the microwave. Pour the butter into a 13 x 9-inch baking pan and tilt the pan to evenly coat the bottom with the butter.

3. In a food processor, process the chocolate wafers to fine crumbs. Sprinkle the crumbs evenly over the butter in the baking pan.

4. Stir the vanilla into the condensed milk and pour evenly over the crumbs in the pan.

5. Sprinkle the apricots, pecans, and chocolate chips evenly on top of the condensed milk.

6. Bake for 30 to 35 minutes, or until lightly browned. Cool in the pan on a rack, then cut into 32 bars.

Golden Nugget Bars

MAKES 16

¾ CUP SUGAR

⅓ CUP BUTTER

½ TEASPOON VANILLA EXTRACT

⅔ CUP FLOUR

1 TEASPOON BAKING POWDER

¼ TEASPOON SALT

1 EGG

1 CUP SEMISWEET CHOCOLATE CHIPS

1 CUP DRY-ROASTED PEANUTS,
    COARSELY CHOPPED

1. Preheat the oven to 375°. Grease and flour an 8-inch square baking pan.

2. In a medium saucepan, combine the sugar and butter, and warm over medium heat until the butter is melted. Remove from the heat and stir in the vanilla. Set aside to cool slightly.

3. Meanwhile, in a medium bowl, thoroughly blend the flour, baking powder, and salt.

4. When the butter mixture has cooled to at least to lukewarm, break the egg into the saucepan and stir immediately to blend.

5. Blend the flour mixture into the saucepan. Stir in the chocolate chips and peanuts.

6. Spread the batter evenly in the prepared pan and bake for 25 minutes, or until a toothpick inserted in the center comes out clean.

7. Cool in the pan on a rack before cutting into 16 bars.

Variation: *These quick, wonderfully rich bar cookies are a sure-fire family favorite, especially if you vary the "mix-ins": Try peanut-butter chips instead of chocolate, or walnuts instead of peanuts. Or replace both the chips and nuts with candy-coated chocolate pieces.*

Toffee-Coconut Bars

MAKES 3 DOZEN

1 STICK BUTTER, AT ROOM
   TEMPERATURE
1½ CUPS LIGHT BROWN SUGAR
1 CUP PLUS 2 TABLESPOONS FLOUR
2 EGGS

1 TEASPOON BAKING POWDER
½ TEASPOON SALT
1 TEASPOON VANILLA EXTRACT
1 CUP SHREDDED COCONUT
1 CUP CHOPPED ALMONDS

1. Preheat the oven to 350°.

2. In a medium bowl, cream the butter and ½ cup of the sugar until fluffy. Gradually add 1 cup of the flour and beat until smooth.

3. Press the dough into a 13 x 9 x 2-inch baking pan. Bake for 10 minutes. Cool slightly.

4. Meanwhile, in a large bowl, beat the eggs. Add the remaining cup of brown sugar, the re-maining 2 tablespoons flour, the baking powder, salt, and vanilla, and stir until combined. Fold in the coconut and almonds.

5. Spread the coconut-almond topping over the baked layer. Bake for 25 minutes, or until golden brown. Cool on a rack, then cut into bars.

KITCHEN NOTE: *For quick cleanup, line the pan with foil. Place the foil in the pan dull side up, and press it gently but firmly into the angles and corners of the pan.*

Mocha-Pecan Bars

MAKES 16

4 OUNCES CHOCOLATE CHIPS

1 STICK BUTTER

1⅔ CUPS DARK BROWN SUGAR

3 TEASPOONS INSTANT ESPRESSO
POWDER OR INSTANT COFFEE
GRANULES

1 CUP FLOUR

½ TEASPOON BAKING POWDER

3 EGGS

1 TEASPOON VANILLA EXTRACT

1 CUP PECAN HALVES, FINELY CHOPPED

¾ CUP POWDERED SUGAR

2 TABLESPOONS COCOA POWDER

2 TABLESPOONS HOT WATER

1. Preheat the oven to 375°. Grease and flour a 13 x 9-inch baking pan.

2. In a large heatproof bowl set over a saucepan of simmering water, melt the chocolate chips with the butter.

3. Remove the bowl of chocolate from the saucepan and stir in the brown sugar and 2 teaspoons of the espresso powder. Stir to dissolve the sugar. Set the chocolate mixture aside to cool slightly.

4. In a small bowl, blend the flour and baking powder. In another small bowl, beat the eggs until frothy.

5. Stir the eggs and vanilla into the chocolate mixture. Stir in the flour mixture and the pecans. Scrape the batter into the prepared baking pan and bake for 20 to 25 minutes, or until a toothpick inserted in the center comes out clean. Let cool in the pan on a rack.

6. In a small bowl, combine the powdered sugar and cocoa. Dissolve the remaining 1 teaspoon espresso powder in the hot water and add to the sugar and cocoa, stirring to blend. Drizzle the glaze over the cooled cake. Let the glaze set before cutting into 16 bars.

BROWNIE CHEESECAKE BARS

MAKES 15

1 CUP FLOUR

⅓ CUP COCOA POWDER

1 TEASPOON BAKING POWDER

4 TABLESPOONS BUTTER, AT ROOM
  TEMPERATURE

⅔ CUP SUGAR

3 EGGS

¼ CUP MILK

ONE 8-OUNCE PACKAGE CREAM
  CHEESE, AT ROOM TEMPERATURE

⅓ CUP SOUR CREAM

½ TEASPOON VANILLA EXTRACT

⅔ CUP SLICED ALMONDS

1. Preheat the oven to 350°. Grease an 8-inch square baking pan, line it with a square of greased wax paper, then flour the pan.

2. In a small bowl, stir together the flour, cocoa, and baking powder.

3. In a large bowl, cream the butter with ⅓ cup of the sugar. Beat in 2 of the eggs, 1 at a time, beating well after each addition. Alternating between the 2, gradually add the flour mixture and the milk, beating well after each addition.

4. Spread the batter evenly in the prepared pan. Rap the pan once or twice on the counter to remove any air pockets. Bake for 10 minutes, or until just set.

5. Meanwhile, in a medium bowl, beat the cream cheese and the remaining sugar until smooth. Beat in the remaining egg, the sour cream, and vanilla.

6. Pour the cream cheese mixture evenly over the brownie layer, spreading it with a rubber spatula. Sprinkle the almonds evenly over the cream cheese layer and bake for another 20 to 25 minutes, or until the cream cheese layer is set.

7. Let cool completely in the pan on a rack, then cut into 15 bars.

CAKES

White Fruitcake

MAKES 6 mini LOAVES

2 CUPS GOLDEN RAISINS

1 CUP DRIED APRICOTS

1 CUP MIXED DRIED FRUIT

1 CUP BRANDY

2 CUPS FLOUR

2 TEASPOONS BAKING POWDER

1 TEASPOON SALT

2 STICKS BUTTER

1 CUP SUGAR

8 EGGS

2 CUPS SLIVERED ALMONDS

2 TEASPOONS GRATED LEMON ZEST

2 TEASPOONS VANILLA EXTRACT

6 TABLESPOONS BOURBON

1. In a medium bowl, combine the raisins, apricots, and dried fruit, and pour the brandy over them. Set aside to soak for at least 4 hours, or overnight.

2. Preheat the oven to 325°. Grease six 5½ x 3 x 2-inch mini loaf pans.

3. In a small bowl, combine the flour, baking powder, and salt; set aside.

4. In a large bowl, cream the butter and sugar until light and fluffy. Beat in the eggs, 1 at a time. Alternating among the 3, stir in the flour mixture, the fruit-brandy mixture, and the almonds, beating well after each addition. Blend in the lemon zest and vanilla.

5. Divide the batter evenly among the prepared pans (they will be nearly full). Rap the pans once or twice on the counter to remove any air pockets. (For easier handling, place the pans on a large baking sheet.) Bake for 45 to 50 minutes, or until the cakes shrink from the sides of the pans and a toothpick inserted in the center of each cake comes out clean.

6. Let the cakes cool in the pans on racks for 30 minutes, then turn them out onto the racks to cool completely.

7. Pour 1 tablespoon of bourbon over each cake and let stand for at least 4 hours. If not serving immediately, wrap each cake in a bourbon-soaked cheesecloth, then in plastic wrap, and store in a tightly closed container.

Dark Gingerbread

SERVES 6 TO 8

2 CUPS FLOUR

1 TABLESPOON COCOA POWDER

1½ TEASPOONS BAKING SODA

2½ TEASPOONS GROUND GINGER

½ TEASPOON ALLSPICE

¼ TEASPOON SALT

⅔ CUP MOLASSES

⅔ CUP SOUR CREAM

1 STICK BUTTER, AT ROOM
  TEMPERATURE

½ CUP DARK BROWN SUGAR

2 EGGS, LIGHTLY BEATEN

1. Preheat the oven to 350°. Grease and flour a 9-inch square baking pan.

2. In a small bowl, stir together the flour, cocoa, baking soda, ginger, allspice, and salt. In another small bowl, stir together the molasses and sour cream.

3. In a large bowl, cream the butter and sugar until smooth. Add the eggs and beat until blended. Alternating between the 2, add the flour mixture and the molasses mixture, beating well after each addition.

4. Spread the batter evenly in the prepared pan. Rap the pan once or twice on the counter to remove any air pockets. Bake for 30 to 35 minutes, or until the cake shrinks from the sides of the pan and a toothpick inserted in the center of the gingerbread comes out clean.

5. Let the gingerbread cool in the pan on a rack, then cut it into squares and serve warm, or at room temperature.

KITCHEN NOTE: *Good as it is with just a glass of milk, homemade gingerbread is even better with a creamy accompaniment. Try a dollop of whipped cream or vanilla yogurt atop each square, or serve the warm gingerbread with scoops of vanilla ice cream.*

YULE LOG CAKE ROLL

SERVES 10

1 CUP FLOUR

4 TEASPOONS CORNSTARCH

1¼ TEASPOONS BAKING POWDER

¼ TEASPOON SALT

4 EGGS, SEPARATED

1 CUP GRANULATED SUGAR

3 TABLESPOONS COLD WATER

½ TEASPOON VANILLA EXTRACT

¾ CUP ORANGE MARMALADE

9 OUNCES SEMISWEET CHOCOLATE,
   CUT INTO PIECES

1¼ CUPS SOUR CREAM

2 TABLESPOONS POWDERED SUGAR

½ TEASPOON MAPLE EXTRACT

CANDIED CHERRIES

CANDIED GREEN CITRON

1. Preheat the oven to 350°. Grease the bottom and sides of a 10½ x 15½-inch jelly-roll pan. Line the pan with a 20-inch strip of wax paper and let the extra paper extend over the ends. Grease and flour the wax paper.

2. In a small bowl, combine the flour, cornstarch, baking powder, and salt; set aside.

3. In a medium bowl, beat the egg whites until they begin to thicken. Slowly add ½ cup of the granulated sugar, beating until stiff peaks form. Beat in the vanilla.

4. In a large bowl, beat the egg yolks, the remaining ½ cup granulated sugar, and the water until thickened. Gradually beat in the flour mixture, beating well after each addition. Gently fold in the egg whites.

5. Pour the batter into the prepared pan and bake for 20 minutes, or until the cake begins to shrink away from the sides of the pan and it springs back instantly when pressed lightly. Carefully turn the cake out on wax paper, peel the layer of paper from the top, and let it rest for 5 minutes, then spread the surface with marmalade. Starting at 1 long edge, roll the cake into a cylinder; set aside to cool.

6. In the top of a double boiler, over hot, not simmering, water, melt the chocolate, stirring until smooth. Set aside to cool slightly. Stir in the sour cream, powdered sugar, and maple extract. Set the frosting aside to cool.

7. Spread the frosting over the entire cake roll. With fork tines, make irregular lines the length of the roll to give the icing a barklike look and the cake the appearance of a log. Decorate the cake with holly berries made from the cherries and with leaf shapes cut from the citron.

SPICE CAKE

SERVES 6 TO 8

¾ CUP HONEY
2 TEASPOONS CINNAMON
4 TEASPOONS GROUND CLOVES
¼ TEASPOON NUTMEG
1 TEASPOON BAKING SODA
2 CUPS FLOUR
¼ TEASPOON SALT
1 TEASPOON BAKING POWDER

⅔ CUP RAISINS
⅓ CUP DRIED CURRANTS
½ CUP FINELY CHOPPED WALNUTS
4 TABLESPOONS UNSALTED BUTTER, AT
    ROOM TEMPERATURE
½ CUP DARK BROWN SUGAR
3 EGGS, SEPARATED

1. Preheat the oven to 300°. Grease and flour the bottom and sides of a 9 x 5 x 3-inch loaf pan.

2. In a small saucepan, bring the honey to a boil over medium heat, stirring constantly. Stir in the cinnamon, cloves, nutmeg, and baking soda, and set aside to cool to room temperature.

3. In a small bowl, combine 1¾ cups of flour with the salt and baking powder; set aside. In another small bowl, combine the raisins, currants, and walnuts with ¼ cup of flour and toss to coat.

4. In a large bowl, cream the butter and sugar until light and fluffy. Beat in the egg yolks, 1 at a time, and stir in the cooled, spiced honey.

Gradually beat in the flour mixture, beating well after each addition. Fold in the fruit-nut mixture until just combined.

5. In another large bowl, beat the egg whites until stiff peaks form. Gently fold the egg whites into the batter.

6. Pour the batter into the prepared pan and bake for 1½ hours, or until a toothpick inserted into the center of the cake comes out clean. With a knife, loosen the sides of the cake from the pan and invert the cake onto a rack. Let the cake cool to room temperature, then cover loosely with wax paper. For the best flavor, set the cake aside for 1 or 2 days at room temperature before slicing.

RASPBERRY CHEESECAKE WITH CHOCOLATE CRUST

SERVES 6 TO 8

ONE 8-OUNCE PACKAGE CHOCOLATE
    WAFERS
⅓ CUP BUTTER, MELTED
TWO 8-OUNCE PACKAGES CREAM
    CHEESE, AT ROOM TEMPERATURE
¾ CUP SUGAR

1 TABLESPOON FLOUR
1 CUP SOUR CREAM
3 EGGS
3 TABLESPOONS FRESH LEMON JUICE
2 TEASPOONS VANILLA EXTRACT
¼ CUP SEEDLESS RASPBERRY JAM

1. Preheat the oven to 350°.

2. In a food processor or blender, process the chocolate wafers to fine crumbs; transfer to a bowl. Add the melted butter and stir to combine, then pat the crumb mixture into the bottom and halfway up the sides of an 8½-inch springform pan; set aside.

3. In a medium bowl, beat the cream cheese and sugar until smooth. Beat in the flour, then the sour cream. Beat in the eggs, 1 at a time, beating well after each addition.

4. Add the lemon juice and vanilla, and beat until smooth. Pour the filling into the crust (the filling will rise above the crust). Bake for 1 to 1¼ hours, or until the filling is set. Let the cake cool completely in a pan on a rack.

5. To serve, place the pan on a serving platter and remove the rim of the pan. Warm the jam in a small saucepan over low heat just until it is pourable. Spoon the jam over the top of the cake.

POPPYSEED CAKE

SERVES 8 TO 10

3 CUPS FLOUR
1½ TEASPOONS BAKING POWDER
½ TEASPOON SALT
3 STICKS BUTTER, AT ROOM
   TEMPERATURE
1½ CUPS GRANULATED SUGAR
5 EGGS

2 TEASPOONS VANILLA EXTRACT
½ CUP POPPY SEEDS
1 CUP SOUR CREAM
⅔ CUP SIFTED POWDERED SUGAR
ABOUT 1 TABLESPOON FRESH LEMON
   JUICE

1. Preheat the oven to 350°. Grease and flour a Bundt pan or 10-inch tube pan.

2. In a medium bowl, stir together the flour, baking powder, and salt; set aside.

3. In a large bowl, cream the butter and granulated sugar until light and fluffy. Beat in the eggs, 1 at a time, beating well after each addition; then beat in the vanilla and the poppy seeds. Alternating between the 2, gradually add the flour mixture and the sour cream, beating well after each addition.

4. Spread the batter in the prepared pan. Rap the pan once or twice on the counter to remove any air pockets. Bake for 50 to 55 minutes, or until the top of the cake springs back when touched, and a toothpick inserted in the center of the cake comes out clean. Let the cake cool in the pan on a rack for 10 minutes, then turn it out onto the rack to cool completely.

5. Meanwhile, in a small bowl, stir together the powdered sugar and lemon juice until smooth. Add up to 1 teaspoon more lemon juice, if necessary, to make it pourable. Place the cake on a serving dish, rounded-side up, and drizzle the glaze over the top.

Mississippi Mud Cake

SERVES 8 TO 10

¼ CUP COCOA POWDER PLUS EXTRA
   FOR DUSTING THE PAN
4 OUNCES UNSWEETENED CHOCOLATE
2 STICKS BUTTER
1½ CUPS STRONG BREWED COFFEE
¼ CUP BOURBON

1¾ CUPS FLOUR
½ TEASPOON BAKING SODA
⅛ TEASPOON SALT
1½ CUPS SUGAR
2 EGGS
1 TEASPOON VANILLA EXTRACT

1. Preheat the oven to 325°. Grease a Bundt pan or 10-inch tube pan and dust it with some cocoa powder.

2. Cut the chocolate into large pieces. In the top of a double boiler, combine the chocolate, butter, coffee, and bourbon. Heat over hot, not simmering, water, stirring occasionally, until the butter and chocolate are melted.

3. Meanwhile, in a medium bowl, stir together the flour, cocoa, baking soda, and salt. Set aside.

4. When the chocolate mixture is melted and smooth, transfer it to a large bowl. Beat at low speed and begin adding the sugar, a little at a time, and continue beating until the sugar is thoroughly incorporated. Gradually beat in the flour mixture, beating well after each addition. Beat in the eggs, 1 at a time, and the vanilla, and beat until smooth.

5. Spread the batter evenly in the prepared pan. Rap the pan once on the counter to remove any air pockets. Bake for 40 to 45 minutes, or until the cake shrinks from the sides of the pan and a toothpick inserted in the center of the cake comes out clean.

6. Let the cake cool completely in the pan on a rack before turning it out onto a serving plate.

MARBLE SPICE CAKE

SERVES 8 TO 10

2 OUNCES SEMISWEET CHOCOLATE

1¾ CUPS MILK

1 TABLESPOON FRESH LEMON JUICE

4½ CUPS CAKE FLOUR

1 TEASPOON BAKING SODA

1 TEASPOON ALLSPICE

1 TEASPOON GROUND GINGER

2 STICKS BUTTER, AT ROOM
  TEMPERATURE

¾ CUP DARK BROWN SUGAR

4 EGGS, SEPARATED

⅓ CUP MOLASSES

2 TEASPOONS BAKING POWDER

¾ CUP GRANULATED SUGAR

1 TEASPOON VANILLA EXTRACT

1 CUP FINELY CHOPPED ALMONDS

I. Preheat the oven to 350°. Generously grease and flour a 10-inch tube pan.

2. In the top of a double boiler, over hot, not simmering, water, melt the chocolate in ¼ cup of milk, stirring until smooth. Set aside.

3. In a cup, stir together ¾ cup of milk and the lemon juice; set aside. In a medium bowl, combine 2 cups of the flour, the baking soda, allspice, and ginger. In a large bowl, cream 1 stick of the butter and brown sugar until light and fluffy. Beat in the egg yolks, 1 at a time, then beat in the molasses and the chocolate mixture. Alternating between the 2, add the flour mixture and the lemon-milk mixture, beating well after each addition. Set the dark batter aside.

4. In a medium bowl, combine the remaining 2½ cups flour and the baking powder. In a large bowl, cream the remaining stick of butter and the granulated sugar until light and fluffy. Add the egg whites, 1 at a time, beating well after each addition. Alternating between the 2, add the flour mixture and the remaining ¾ cup milk, beating well after each addition. Add the vanilla and almonds and stir until blended.

5. Using two ¼-cup measures, scoop a portion of each batter into the prepared pan. Alternate scoops of each batter, placing dark batter on light and light on dark. Repeat until all the batter is used.

6. Bake for 1¼ hours, or until a toothpick inserted in the center of the cake comes out clean. Let the cake cool in the pan on a rack for 10 minutes, then turn it out onto the rack to cool completely.

BUTTER-RUM CAKE

SERVES 6 TO 8

1½ CUPS FLOUR

½ CUP YELLOW CORNMEAL

2 TEASPOONS BAKING POWDER

1 STICK BUTTER, AT ROOM
   TEMPERATURE

1 CUP SUGAR

4 EGGS

¼ CUP DARK RUM

3 TABLESPOONS FRESH LIME JUICE

1 TEASPOON GRATED LIME ZEST

POWDERED SUGAR (OPTIONAL)

1. Preheat the oven to 350°. Grease and flour the bottom and sides of an 8-inch springform cake pan.

2. Sift the flour, cornmeal, and baking powder into a bowl; set aside.

3. In a large bowl, cream the butter and sugar until light and fluffy. Beat in the eggs, 1 at a time, then add the rum, lime juice, and lime zest, and continue beating until the batter is smooth. Add the flour mixture, ½ cup at a time, beating well after each addition.

4. Pour the batter into the prepared pan and bake for 1 hour, or until a toothpick inserted in the center of the cake comes out clean. Cool the cake completely before removing the sides of the pan.

5. Sift a light coating of powdered sugar over the top of the cooled cake before serving, if desired.

KITCHEN NOTE: *This festive cake makes a wonderful dinner-party dessert. To dress it up for the occasion, sift the powdered sugar on the cake over a doily.*

Ginger Angel Food Cake with Berry Sauce

SERVES 8 TO 10

1 CUP CAKE FLOUR

1¾ CUPS PLUS 2 TABLESPOONS SUGAR

16 LARGE EGG WHITES, AT ROOM
TEMPERATURE

1 TEASPOON CREAM OF TARTAR

½ TEASPOON SALT

1 TABLESPOON MINCED FRESH GINGER

1 TEASPOON VANILLA EXTRACT

2 CUPS FRESH OR FROZEN THAWED
STRAWBERRIES

2 CUPS FRESH OR FROZEN THAWED
RASPBERRIES

2 CUPS FRESH OR FROZEN THAWED
BLUEBERRIES

WHIPPED CREAM (OPTIONAL)

1. Preheat the oven to 325°.

2. Sift the flour and ½ cup of the sugar 3 times; set aside.

3. In a large bowl, beat the egg whites, cream of tartar, and salt until soft peaks form. Very gradually beat in 1¼ cups of sugar, then continue beating until stiff peaks form; they should look glossy, not dry.

4. Sift about ¼ cup of the flour mixture over the beaten egg whites, then fold in, using a rubber spatula. Fold in the ginger and the vanilla, then fold in the remaining flour mixture, ¼ cup at a time.

5. Spread the batter evenly in a 10-inch tube pan with a removable bottom. Rap the pan once on the counter to remove any air pock-

ets. Bake for 40 minutes, or until the cake shrinks from the sides of the pan, and a toothpick inserted in the center of the cake comes out clean.

6. Turn the pan upside down (if your pan does not have "legs," slip the tube of the pan over the neck of a bottle). Let the cake cool, upside down, for 1½ hours, then run a knife around the edge of the pan and pull off the sides of the pan. Run a knife around the tube and the bottom of the pan and turn the cake out onto a plate.

7. Place half of the strawberries, raspberries, and blueberries in a bowl and gently mash them. Stir in the remaining sugar, then fold in the remaining berries. Serve the cake with the berry topping, and whipped cream, if desired.

Chocolate-Mocha Roll

SERVES 8

1 CUP HEAVY CREAM
1 TABLESPOON INSTANT COFFEE
3 OUNCES SEMISWEET CHOCOLATE
⅓ CUP CAKE FLOUR
¼ CUP COCOA POWDER
¼ TEASPOON BAKING POWDER

¼ TEASPOON SALT
4 EGGS, SEPARATED
1 TEASPOON VANILLA EXTRACT
PINCH OF CREAM OF TARTAR
⅔ CUP GRANULATED SUGAR
1 TABLESPOON POWDERED SUGAR

1. In a small saucepan, combine the cream and coffee and stir to dissolve. Add the chocolate and warm over medium-low heat, stirring occasionally, until the chocolate is melted. Cover and refrigerate the mocha cream at least 3 hours.

2. Preheat the oven to 400°. Grease the bottom of a 15½ x 10½-inch jelly-roll pan. Line the bottom with wax paper. Grease and flour the wax paper.

3. In a small bowl, combine the flour, cocoa powder, baking powder, and salt. In a medium bowl, beat together the egg yolks and vanilla. Stir in half of the flour mixture.

4. In a large bowl, beat the egg whites until frothy. Add the cream of tartar and continue beating until soft peaks form. Gradually add the granulated sugar and continue beating until stiff peaks form. Fold the egg whites into the egg yolk mixture. Sprinkle the rest of the flour mixture over the egg mixture and gently fold them in. Immediately spread the batter in the prepared pan and bake for 8 to 10 minutes, or until the top of the cake springs back when pressed.

5. Carefully remove the wax paper from the cake. Starting with a short side, roll the cake into a log. Set the cake aside to cool.

6. Place the bowl of chilled mocha cream in the freezer for 5 minutes. Beat the mocha cream until stiff peaks form.

7. Gently unroll the cake (do not flatten it completely or it will crack). Gently spread the whipped mocha cream over the cake, leaving a 1-inch border. Starting with a short side, carefully reroll the cake. If not serving immediately, cover well and refrigerate. Before serving, trim off the ends of the cake and sprinkle with the powdered sugar.

DUNDEE CAKE

SERVES 6 TO 8

2 STICKS BUTTER, AT ROOM
   TEMPERATURE
1 CUP SUGAR
5 EGGS, LIGHTLY BEATEN
2½ CUPS FLOUR
¾ CUP DRIED CURRANTS
¾ CUP SEEDLESS RAISINS
¾ CUP COARSELY CHOPPED MIXED
   CANDIED FRUIT PEEL

8 CANDIED CHERRIES, CUT IN HALF
½ CUP GROUND ALMONDS
2 TABLESPOONS GRATED ORANGE ZEST
PINCH OF SALT
1 TEASPOON BAKING SODA DISSOLVED
   IN 1 TEASPOON MILK
⅓ CUP ALMONDS, SPLIT LENGTHWISE
   INTO HALVES

1. Preheat the oven to 300°. Grease and flour the bottom and sides of an 8 x 3-inch springform cake pan.

2. In a large bowl, cream the butter and sugar until light and fluffy. Alternating between the 2, beat in the eggs and flour, beating well after each addition. Beat in the currants, raisins, candied fruit peel, cherries, ground almonds, orange zest, and salt, and continue beating until well combined. Stir in the dissolved baking soda, pour the batter into the prepared pan, and arrange the split almonds on top in concentric circles.

3. Bake for 1½ hours, or until a toothpick inserted in the center of the cake comes out clean. Let the cake cool in the pan on a rack for 4 to 5 minutes before removing the sides of the pan.

KITCHEN NOTE: *This wonderful old-fashioned Scottish cake calls for candied peel, which is not as common an ingredient as it once was, but you can often find good-quality candied orange and lemon peel at gourmet shops and candy stores.*

DARK CHOCOLATE BUNDT CAKE

SERVES 8 TO 10

½ CUP PLUS 2 TABLESPOONS COCOA
POWDER
8 OUNCES SEMISWEET CHOCOLATE,
CUT INTO PIECES
2 CUPS FLOUR
1½ TEASPOONS BAKING POWDER
¼ TEASPOON SALT

2 STICKS BUTTER, AT ROOM
TEMPERATURE
1½ CUPS BROWN SUGAR
4 EGGS
1½ TEASPOONS VANILLA EXTRACT
1 CUP PLUS 1 TABLESPOON MILK
¾ CUP POWDERED SUGAR

1. Preheat the oven to 350°. Grease a Bundt pan or 10-inch tube pan and dust it with 2 tablespoons of the cocoa powder.

2. In a double boiler, melt the chocolate over hot, not simmering, water, stirring occasionally, until smooth. Set aside to cool slightly.

3. Meanwhile, in a medium bowl, combine the flour, the remaining ½ cup cocoa, the baking powder, and salt. Set aside.

4. In a large bowl, cream the butter and brown sugar until light and fluffy. Beat in the eggs, 1 at a time, then beat in the vanilla. Add the melted chocolate and beat until blended.

5. Alternating between the 2, gradually add the flour mixture and 1 cup of milk, beating just until blended; do not overbeat.

6. Spread the batter in the prepared pan. Rap the pan a few times on the counter to remove any air pockets. Bake for 55 to 60 minutes, or until the top of the cake springs back when touched, and a toothpick inserted in the center of the cake comes out clean. Let the cake cool in the pan on a rack for 15 minutes.

7. Meanwhile, in a small bowl, stir together the powdered sugar and the remaining tablespoon of milk until smooth and pourable.

8. Turn the cake out onto a serving dish, rounded-side up, and drizzle the glaze over the top.

BOURBON POUND CAKE

SERVES 8 TO 10

2 CUPS RAISINS

½ CUP BOURBON

2 CUPS FLOUR

1 TEASPOON NUTMEG

¾ TEASPOON BAKING SODA

¼ TEASPOON SALT

1½ STICKS BUTTER, AT ROOM
    TEMPERATURE

½ CUP DARK BROWN SUGAR

½ CUP GRANULATED SUGAR

4 EGGS

½ CUP MOLASSES

1 TEASPOON VANILLA EXTRACT

2 CUPS CHOPPED PECANS, PLUS ¾ CUP
    PECAN HALVES

1. Preheat the oven to 350°. Grease a 10-inch tube pan and line the bottom with a ring of wax paper. Grease the wax paper.

2. Place the raisins in a small bowl with ¼ cup of the bourbon. Set aside to soak for 1 hour, stirring occasionally. Reserving the bourbon, drain the raisins; set aside.

3. In a small bowl, stir together the flour, nutmeg, baking soda, and salt.

4. In a large bowl, cream the butter, brown sugar, and granulated sugar. Add the eggs, 1 at a time, beating well after each addition. Add the molasses, vanilla, and the reserved bourbon. Gradually add the flour mixture, beating well after each addition. Fold in the chopped pecans and the drained raisins.

5. Spread the batter evenly in the prepared pan. Rap the pan once or twice on the counter to remove any air pockets. Arrange the pecan halves decoratively on top of the batter and bake for 50 to 55 minutes, or until the cake shrinks from the sides of the pan and a toothpick inserted into the center of the cake comes out clean.

6. Let the cake cool in the pan for 30 minutes. Turn the cake out onto a plate and remove the wax paper. Then invert the cake onto a rack, right-side up, to cool completely.

7. Place the cake in an airtight container and drape a sheet of cheesecloth over the cake. Slowly pour the remaining ¼ cup of bourbon over the cloth and cake and store in a tightly closed container.

Boston Cream Pie

1¾ CUPS CAKE FLOUR

2 TEASPOONS BAKING POWDER

¾ TEASPOON SALT

⅓ CUP PLUS 2 TABLESPOONS BUTTER, AT ROOM TEMPERATURE

1 CUP GRANULATED SUGAR

2½ TEASPOONS VANILLA EXTRACT

3 EGGS PLUS 1 EGG YOLK

⅓ CUP MILK

1 CUP PLUS 2 TABLESPOONS LIGHT CREAM OR HALF-AND-HALF

¼ CUP ALL-PURPOSE FLOUR

2 OUNCES UNSWEETENED CHOCOLATE

½ CUP LIGHT BROWN SUGAR

1. Preheat the oven to 350°. Grease and flour two 8-inch round cake pans.

2. In a small bowl, combine the cake flour, baking powder, and ½ teaspoon of the salt.

3. In a large bowl, cream ⅓ cup of butter and ¾ cup of granulated sugar. Beat in 1 teaspoon of vanilla. Beat in 2 of the eggs, 1 at a time, beating well after each addition. Gradually beat in the flour mixture and the milk.

4. Spread the batter in the prepared pans. Bake for 20 minutes, or until a toothpick inserted in the center of the cakes comes out clean. Cool the cakes in the pans for 10 minutes before turning them out onto a rack.

5. In a small saucepan, scald 1 cup of the cream. In a medium bowl, combine the remaining ¼ cup of granulated sugar, the all-purpose flour, and the remaining ¼ teaspoon of salt. Pour in the hot cream and stir the mixture until smooth.

6. In the top of a double boiler, beat the remaining egg and egg yolk together. Slowly pour in the hot cream-flour mixture and cook over boiling water, stirring constantly, until the custard thickens, about 5 minutes. Remove from the heat and stir in 1 teaspoon of vanilla. Let cool, cover, and refrigerate.

7. In the top of a double boiler, melt the chocolate over hot, not simmering, water. Remove from the heat and cool slightly.

8. In a medium bowl, cream the remaining 2 tablespoons butter and ½ teaspoon vanilla. Gradually beat in the brown sugar, 2 tablespoons cream, and the melted chocolate. Continue beating until the frosting is stiff.

9. Spread the custard filling over 1 cake layer. Top with the second layer and frost the top of the cake with the chocolate frosting. Chill (to set the frosting) until ready to serve.

CHOCOLATE-ALMOND TORTE

SERVES 6 TO 8

1 CUP ALMONDS
1½ CUPS POWDERED SUGAR
3 EGGS PLUS 1 EGG WHITE
⅔ CUP FLOUR
⅓ CUP COCOA POWDER
½ TEASPOON BAKING POWDER

1½ STICKS BUTTER, AT ROOM
   TEMPERATURE
½ TEASPOON ALMOND EXTRACT
2 OUNCES SEMISWEET CHOCOLATE,
   CUT INTO PIECES
¼ CUP HEAVY CREAM

1. Preheat the oven to 350°. Grease an 8 x 2-inch round cake pan, line the bottom with greased wax paper, and then flour the pan.

2. Place the almonds in a food processor and process, pulsing the machine on and off, for 5 to 10 seconds, or just until the almonds are finely ground. Do not overprocess or the nuts will turn into a paste. Add the sugar and egg white, and pulse just until combined; set aside.

3. In a small bowl, combine the flour, cocoa powder, and baking powder; set aside.

4. In a large bowl, combine the almond mixture with the butter and beat until creamy and light. Add the whole eggs, 1 at a time, beating well after each addition, then beat in the almond extract.

5. Gradually add the flour mixture, beating just until combined; do not overbeat.

6. Spread the batter in the prepared pan. Rap the pan once or twice on the counter to remove any air pockets. Bake for 30 to 35 minutes, or until the cake shrinks from the sides of the pan and a toothpick inserted into the center of the cake comes out clean.

7. Let the cake cool in the pan on a rack for 15 minutes, then turn it out onto the rack to cool completely.

8. Meanwhile, place the chocolate and cream in a double boiler and heat over simmering water, stirring often, until the chocolate has melted and the mixture is smooth.

9. Remove the wax paper from the cake, leaving the cake on the rack. Place a large sheet of wax paper under the rack. Pour the glaze onto the center of the cake and tilt the rack to allow the glaze to coat the entire top and sides. Leave the cake on the rack until the glaze has set.

BLACK FOREST CAKE

SERVES 8 TO 10

6 EGGS, AT ROOM TEMPERATURE
1 TEASPOON VANILLA EXTRACT
1 CUP GRANULATED SUGAR
½ CUP FLOUR
½ CUP COCOA POWDER
10 TABLESPOONS UNSALTED BUTTER,
    MELTED

3 CUPS COLD HEAVY CREAM
½ CUP POWDERED SUGAR
1 CUP DRAINED AND RINSED CANNED
    SOUR RED CHERRIES
CHOCOLATE CURLS (OPTIONAL)
MARASCHINO CHERRIES WITH STEMS,
    DRAINED AND RINSED (OPTIONAL)

1. Preheat the oven to 350°. Grease and flour three 7-inch round cake pans.

2. In a large bowl, beat the eggs, vanilla, and granulated sugar at high speed for at least 10 minutes, or until the mixture is thick and fluffy.

3. Combine the flour and cocoa in a sifter. Gradually sift the mixture over the eggs, folding it in gently with a rubber spatula. Stir in the butter, 2 tablespoons at a time, until just combined. Do not overmix. Dividing evenly, gently pour the batter into the prepared cake pans.

4. Bake for 10 to 15 minutes, or until a toothpick inserted in the center of the cakes comes out clean. Let the cakes cool in the pans for about 5 minutes, then run a knife around the edge of each cake and turn them out onto racks to cool completely.

5. In a large chilled bowl, beat the cream until it thickens slightly. Gradually add the powdered sugar and beat until stiff peaks form.

6. Place 1 of the cake layers in the center of a serving plate. Spread the top with a ½-inch-thick layer of the whipped cream. Arrange the cherries on the whipped cream, leaving a ½-inch border. Gently set a second cake layer on top of the cherries and spread it with ½ inch of whipped cream. Set the third layer in place. Spread the top and sides of the cake with the remaining whipped cream.

7. Gently press chocolate curls into the cream on the sides of the cake and arrange a few chocolate curls and maraschino cherries attractively on top, if desired.

LEMON LAYER CAKE

SERVES 6 TO 8

1¾ CUPS FLOUR

1 TEASPOON BAKING POWDER

¼ TEASPOON SALT

7 EGGS, SEPARATED, PLUS 5 EGG YOLKS

1⅔ CUPS PLUS ½ CUP GRANULATED
   SUGAR

¾ CUP FRESH LEMON JUICE

3 TABLESPOONS GRATED LEMON ZEST

½ TEASPOON CREAM OF TARTAR

1 STICK OF BUTTER, AT ROOM
   TEMPERATURE

2 TEASPOONS CORNSTARCH

2½ CUPS POWDERED SUGAR

1. Preheat the oven to 350°. Generously grease and flour two 9-inch round cake pans.

2. In a small bowl, combine the flour, baking powder, and salt. In a large bowl, beat 7 egg yolks and 1⅔ cups granulated sugar until pale and lemon-colored. Beat in ¼ cup of lemon juice and 1 tablespoon of lemon zest. Gradually beat in the flour mixture until well blended.

3. In a medium bowl, beat the 7 egg whites until frothy. Add the cream of tartar and continue beating until stiff peaks form. Gently fold the beaten egg whites into the batter.

4. Spread the batter in the prepared pans. Rap the pans once on the counter to remove any air pockets. Bake for 25 minutes, or until a toothpick inserted into the center of the cakes comes out clean. Let the cakes cool in the pans for 5 minutes, then turn them out onto racks to cool completely.

5. Meanwhile, in a medium saucepan, combine 5 egg yolks, ½ stick of butter, ½ cup granulated sugar, ¼ cup lemon juice, 1 tablespoon lemon zest, and the cornstarch. Stirring constantly, cook over very low heat until the mixture is thick enough to coat the back of a spoon, 15 to 20 minutes. Scrape the filling into a bowl and let it cool.

6. In a medium bowl, cream the remaining ½ stick of butter until light and fluffy. Beat in the remaining ¼ cup of lemon juice and the powdered sugar. Beat in the remaining tablespoon of lemon zest. Set the frosting aside.

7. Cut each cake layer in half horizontally. Place 1 layer cut-side up and spread ⅓ of the lemon filling over it. Put another layer cut-side down on top and spread it with half the remaining filling; repeat with the third layer and the remaining filling. Top with the fourth layer, cut-side down. Spread the frosting over the top and sides of the cake.

BLACKBERRY JAM CAKE

SERVES 6 TO 8

2¼ CUPS FLOUR
1 TEASPOON BAKING SODA
1 TEASPOON CINNAMON
½ TEASPOON NUTMEG
¼ TEASPOON SALT
2½ STICKS BUTTER, AT ROOM
    TEMPERATURE
1 CUP GRANULATED SUGAR
3 EGGS, SEPARATED

⅓ CUP BUTTERMILK OR PLAIN YOGURT
1 CUP BLACKBERRY JAM
1 TABLESPOON PLUS 2 TEASPOONS
    GRATED ORANGE ZEST
½ TEASPOON ORANGE EXTRACT
11 OUNCES CREAM CHEESE, AT ROOM
    TEMPERATURE
1½ TEASPOONS VANILLA EXTRACT
2 CUPS POWDERED SUGAR

1. Preheat the oven the 350°. Grease two 8-inch round cake pans and line the bottoms with circles of wax paper. Grease the wax paper, then flour the pans.

2. In a small bowl, combine the flour, baking soda, cinnamon, nutmeg, and salt; set aside.

3. In a large bowl, cream 1½ sticks of the butter and the granulated sugar until light and fluffy. Beat in the egg yolks, buttermilk, jam, 1 tablespoon of orange zest, and the orange extract. Stir in the flour mixture.

4. In a medium bowl, beat the egg whites until stiff but not dry. Gently fold the egg whites into the batter.

5. Spread the batter evenly in the prepared pans. Rap the pans once or twice on the counter to remove any air pockets. Bake for 45 to 50 minutes, or until the cakes shrink from the sides of the pans and a toothpick inserted into the center of each cake comes out clean. Let the cakes cool in the pans for 10 minutes, then turn them out onto racks to cool completely before frosting.

6. Meanwhile, in a medium bowl, beat the cream cheese and the remaining stick of butter until smooth. Beat in the remaining orange zest and the vanilla. Gradually add the powdered sugar, beating well until the frosting is thick and smooth.

7. Remove the wax paper from the layers. Spread a generous layer of frosting over 1 cake layer. Top with the second layer, then frost the top and sides of the cake.

ALMOND LAYER CAKE WITH RUM GLAZE

SERVES 6 TO 8

1½ CUPS ALMONDS

8 EGGS—2 LEFT WHOLE AND 6
    SEPARATED

½ CUP GRANULATED SUGAR

⅓ CUP FLOUR

2¼ CUPS POWDERED SUGAR

2 TABLESPOONS MILK

2 TABLESPOONS RUM

1 TABLESPOON FRESH LEMON JUICE

½ CUP RASPBERRY OR STRAWBERRY JAM

1. Preheat the oven to 350°. Grease and flour two 8-inch round cake pans.

2. Spread the almonds in a shallow roasting pan or jelly-roll pan and toast them in the oven, turning them occasionally, for about 5 minutes, or until they are golden brown. Pulverize the nuts in an electric blender or with a nut grinder or a mortar and pestle, and set them aside.

3. In a large bowl, beat 2 whole eggs, 6 egg yolks, and the granulated sugar until the mixture is thick enough to fall back on itself in a slowly dissolving ribbon when the beater is lifted from the bowl. Beat in the flour and ground almonds.

4. In a separate bowl, beat the 6 egg whites until stiff peaks form. With a rubber spatula, gently but thoroughly fold the egg whites into the egg yolk batter. Pour the batter into the prepared pans. Bake for 20 minutes, or until a toothpick inserted in the center of the cakes comes out clean. Cool the cakes in the pans for 5 minutes, then run a sharp knife around the outside edges of the cakes, and turn them out onto a rack to cool completely.

5. Meanwhile, in a large bowl, combine the powdered sugar, milk, rum, and lemon juice. Beat for about 5 minutes, or until the glaze is smooth and as thick as heavy cream. If the glaze seems too thin, beat in additional powdered sugar, 1 teaspoon at a time.

6. Place 1 of the cake layers in the center of a large serving platter. Spread the jam over the cake. Set the other layer on top, and coat it with the rum glaze.

German Chocolate Cake

SERVES 8 TO 10

½ CUP WATER

6 OUNCES MILK CHOCOLATE, CUT INTO
PIECES

2½ CUPS CAKE FLOUR

1 TEASPOON BAKING SODA

½ TEASPOON SALT

3 STICKS BUTTER, AT ROOM
TEMPERATURE

2½ CUPS SUGAR

4 EGGS

1½ TEASPOONS VANILLA EXTRACT

1 CUP BUTTERMILK

½ CUP LIGHT BROWN SUGAR

1 CUP HEAVY CREAM

4 OUNCES UNSWEETENED CHOCOLATE,
CUT INTO PIECES

1½ CUPS SHREDDED COCONUT

1 CUP COARSELY CHOPPED PECANS

1. Preheat the oven to 350°. Grease and flour the bottom and sides of three 9-inch cake pans.

2. In a small saucepan, bring the water to a boil. Drop in the milk chocolate, reduce the heat to low, and stir until the chocolate melts and the mixture is smooth. Remove the pan from the heat and let cool.

3. In a medium bowl, combine the flour, baking soda, and salt; set aside. In a large bowl, cream 2 sticks of butter and 1¾ cups of sugar until light and fluffy. Beat in the eggs, 1 at a time, then stir in the vanilla. Stirring constantly, pour in the chocolate mixture in a slow, thin stream and continue to beat until the batter is smooth. Alternating between the 2, gradually add the flour mixture and the buttermilk, beating well after each addition.

4. Pour the batter into the prepared pans. Bake for 35 minutes, or until a toothpick inserted in the center of the cakes comes out clean. Cool for 5 minutes; turn out onto racks.

5. Meanwhile, in a small saucepan, combine the remaining ¾ cup granulated sugar, the brown sugar, and cream, and bring to a boil over medium heat, stirring constantly. Reduce the heat to low and cook, without stirring, for 6 minutes. Remove the pan from the heat, stir in the unsweetened chocolate and the remaining stick of butter until melted. Beat the frosting until cooled, thick, and creamy. Stir in the coconut and pecans.

6. Place 1 cake layer on a serving plate and spread the top with frosting. Set the second layer in place, frost it, then add the third cake layer. Frost the top and sides of the cake with the remaining frosting.

SOUR CREAM POUND CAKE

SERVES 6 TO 8

1 STICK UNSALTED BUTTER, AT ROOM
   TEMPERATURE
1 CUP SUGAR
3 EGGS
1¾ CUPS FLOUR

1 TEASPOON BAKING SODA
½ TEASPOON CINNAMON
1 TEASPOON CARDAMOM
1 CUP SOUR CREAM
1 TEASPOON VANILLA EXTRACT

1. Preheat the oven to 350°. Grease and flour a 9 x 5 x 3-inch loaf pan.

2. In a large bowl, cream the butter and sugar until light and fluffy. Beat in the eggs, 1 at a time, beating well after each addition. Sift together the flour, baking soda, cinnamon, and cardamom and stir half of it into the batter. Beat in the sour cream and vanilla, and when all these ingredients are well combined, beat in the rest of the dry ingredients.

3. Pour the contents of the bowl into the prepared pan and rap the pan sharply on the table once to remove any air pockets. Bake for 50 to 60 minutes, or until the top of the cake is golden brown and is lightly springy to the touch. Run a knife around the cake to loosen it from the pan. Turn the cake out onto a plate, then invert the cake onto a rack, right-side up, to cool.

KITCHEN NOTE: *The secret to fine-grained pound cake is carefully beaten batter, which is easier to achieve if all the ingredients—including the eggs and sour cream—are at room temperature. It's also a good idea to stir the dry ingredients after sifting them together; sifting alone may not distribute the baking soda and spices evenly.*

Chocolate-Cream Cheese Cupcakes

Makes 12

¾ CUP FLOUR

⅓ CUP COCOA POWDER

½ TEASPOON BAKING SODA

⅓ CUP PLUS 2 TABLESPOONS BUTTER,
AT ROOM TEMPERATURE

⅔ CUP PLUS 3 TABLESPOONS
GRANULATED SUGAR

3 EGGS

1 TEASPOON VANILLA EXTRACT

¾ CUP SOUR CREAM

ONE 3-OUNCE PACKAGE CREAM
CHEESE, AT ROOM TEMPERATURE

¼ CUP LIGHT BROWN SUGAR

¼ CUP HEAVY CREAM

1 OUNCE SEMISWEET CHOCOLATE,
BROKEN INTO PIECES

1. Preheat the oven to 350°. Line 12 cupcake tins with paper baking cups.

2. In a medium bowl, stir together the flour, cocoa powder, and baking soda. In a large bowl, cream ⅓ cup of butter and ⅔ cup of the granulated sugar until light and fluffy. Beat in 2 of the eggs, ½ teaspoon of vanilla, and ½ cup of sour cream, beating well after each addition. Add the flour mixture and stir until just blended; do not overbeat. Set the chocolate batter aside.

3. In a medium bowl, beat the cream cheese with the remaining sour cream, granulated sugar, vanilla, and egg. Set the cream cheese batter aside.

4. Divide the chocolate batter evenly among the cupcake tins, filling them no more than half full. Spoon the cream cheese batter on top (the cups will be filled to within ¼ inch of their tops). Bake for 20 to 25 minutes, or until the tops of the cupcakes spring back when touched with a finger. Cool the cupcakes in the pans for 5 minutes, then place them on a rack to cool completely before frosting.

5. Meanwhile, in a small saucepan, bring the brown sugar and cream to a boil, stirring constantly. Reduce the heat so the mixture simmers and cook without stirring for 5 minutes. Remove the pan from the heat, stir in the chocolate and the remaining butter, and stir until melted. Transfer the icing to a medium bowl and beat until it is spreadable and will just hold soft peaks, 7 to 10 minutes.

6. Spread a thick layer of icing on the top of each cupcake.

PIES & PUDDINGS

Mini Mincemeat Pies

SERVES 8

1½ CUPS FLOUR

¼ TEASPOON SALT

1 TABLESPOON SUGAR

6 TABLESPOONS UNSALTED BUTTER, AT
    ROOM TEMPERATURE

2 TABLESPOONS VEGETABLE
    SHORTENING

3 TO 4 TABLESPOONS ICE WATER

1½ CUPS MINCEMEAT

1. Preheat the oven to 375°. Grease the bottom and sides of eight 2½-inch tart tins.

2. In a large bowl, combine the flour, salt, and sugar. With a pastry blender or 2 knives, cut the butter and the shortening into the flour until it is coarse crumbs. Pour 3 tablespoons of ice water over the mixture all at once, toss together lightly, and gather the dough into a ball. If the dough crumbles, add up to 1 tablespoon more ice water by drops until the particles adhere.

3. On a lightly floured surface, roll the dough out to a ⅛-inch thickness. With a cookie cutter or the rim of a glass, cut sixteen 3½-inch rounds of pastry. Gently press 8 of the rounds, 1 at a time, into the tart tins.

4. Spoon about 3 tablespoons of mincemeat into each pastry shell. With a pastry brush dipped in cold water, lightly moisten the outside edges of the pastry shells and carefully fit the remaining 8 rounds over them. Crimp the edges of the pastry together with the tines of a fork. Cut 2 steam vents in the top of each pie.

5. Arrange the pies on a large baking sheet, and bake for 10 minutes. Reduce the oven temperature to 350° and bake for 20 minutes, or until the crust is golden brown. Run the blade of a knife around the inside edges of the pies to loosen them slightly, and set them aside to cool in the pans. Turn out the pies with a narrow spatula and serve.

EGGNOG PIE

SERVES 6 TO 8

1¼ CUPS PLUS 2 TABLESPOONS FLOUR

¾ TEASPOON SALT

1½ STICKS BUTTER, AT ROOM
TEMPERATURE

3 TABLESPOONS VEGETABLE
SHORTENING

4 TO 5 TABLESPOONS ICE WATER

¾ CUP SUGAR

3 EGGS

1 CUP HEAVY CREAM

½ CUP MILK

1 TEASPOON VANILLA EXTRACT

½ TEASPOON NUTMEG

1. In a large bowl, combine 1¼ cups of the flour and the salt. With a pastry blender or 2 knives, cut in 4 tablespoons of butter and the shortening until the mixture resembles coarse crumbs.

2. Sprinkle 4 tablespoons of the ice water over the mixture and toss it with a fork. The dough should be moistened just enough so that it holds together when it is formed into a ball. If necessary, add up to 1 tablespoon more ice water, drop by drop. Shape the dough into a flat disc, wrap in plastic wrap and refrigerate for at least 30 minutes, or until well chilled.

3. On a lightly floured surface, roll the dough into a 12-inch circle. Fit the dough into a 9-inch pie pan. Trim the overhang to an even ½ inch all the way around and fold the dough under; crimp the dough to form a decorative border. Prick the pastry with a fork.

Place the pie shell in the freezer for at least 15 minutes before filling and baking.

4. Preheat the oven to 400°.

5. Line the pie shell with foil, fill it with pie weights or dried beans, and bake for 10 minutes. Remove the foil and weights, and set the pie shell aside to cool; reduce the oven temperature to 375°.

6. In a large bowl, cream the remaining stick of butter and the sugar. Gradually beat in the eggs, cream, milk, vanilla, nutmeg, and the remaining 2 tablespoons flour. Pour the filling into the pie shell and bake for 20 minutes.

7. Reduce the oven temperature to 300° and bake for another 10 minutes, or until the filling is set and golden. Serve the pie warm or at room temperature.

CHOCOLATE-BUTTERSCOTCH PIE

SERVES 6 TO 8

1½ CUPS FLOUR

¼ TEASPOON SALT

6 TABLESPOONS UNSALTED BUTTER, AT ROOM TEMPERATURE

2 TABLESPOONS VEGETABLE SHORTENING

3 TO 4 TABLESPOONS ICE WATER

2 OUNCES UNSWEETENED CHOCOLATE

1 STICK BUTTER, AT ROOM TEMPERATURE

2 CUPS LIGHT BROWN SUGAR

3 EGGS

1 TEASPOON VANILLA EXTRACT

½ CUP LIGHT CREAM OR HALF-AND-HALF

2 CUPS SWEETENED WHIPPED CREAM

1. Preheat the oven to 400°

2. In a large bowl, combine the flour and salt. With a pastry blender or 2 knives, cut the unsalted butter and the shortening into the flour until it resembles coarse crumbs. Pour 3 tablespoons of ice water over the mixture all at once, toss together lightly, and gather the dough into a ball. If the dough crumbles, add up to 1 tablespoon more ice water by drops until the particles adhere.

3. On a lightly floured surface, roll the dough into a 12-inch circle. Fit the dough into a 9-inch pie pan. Trim the overhang to an even 1 inch and fold the dough under; crimp the dough to form a decorative border. Prick the pastry with a fork. Line the pie shell with foil, fill it with pie weights or dried beans, and bake for 10 minutes. Remove the crust from the oven and reduce the temperature to 350°.

4. Meanwhile, in a small saucepan, melt the chocolate over very low heat, stirring frequently. Set aside to cool.

5. In a large bowl, cream the stick of butter and the sugar until light and fluffy. Beat in the eggs, 1 at a time, then stir in the vanilla, light cream, and melted chocolate. Pour the filling into the pastry shell and bake for 45 to 50 minutes, or until the filling is set. Cool the pie to room temperature. Spread the sweetened whipped cream on the surface of the cooled pie and serve at once.

CRANBERRY-PECAN PIE

SERVES 6 TO 8

1¼ CUPS FLOUR

⅓ CUP CORNMEAL

2 TABLESPOONS SUGAR

¾ TEASPOON SALT

4 TABLESPOONS BUTTER, AT ROOM
  TEMPERATURE

3 TABLESPOONS VEGETABLE
  SHORTENING

4 TO 5 TABLESPOONS ICE WATER

3 CUPS CRANBERRIES, COARSELY
  CHOPPED

2 MEDIUM APPLES, FINELY CHOPPED

¾ CUP DRIED APRICOTS, CHOPPED

¾ CUP CHOPPED PECANS

⅓ CUP MAPLE SYRUP

1 EGG YOLK BEATEN WITH
  1 TABLESPOON MILK

⅓ CUP ORANGE MARMALADE

1. In a large bowl, combine 1 cup of the flour, the cornmeal, sugar, and salt. With a pastry blender or 2 knives, cut in the butter and shortening until the mixture resembles coarse crumbs.

2. Sprinkle 2 tablespoons of ice water over the mixture and toss it with a fork. The dough should be just barely moistened, enough so it will hold together when it is formed into a ball. If necessary, add up to 3 tablespoons more ice water, 1 tablespoon at a time.

3. On a lightly floured surface, roll the dough out to a 12-inch circle. Fit the dough into a 9-inch pie pan. Trim the overhang to an even ½ inch and fold it under; crimp the dough to form a decorative border. Prick the pastry with a fork.

4. Preheat the oven to 400°.

5. In a large bowl, combine the cranberries, apples, apricots, pecans, maple syrup, and the remaining ¼ cup flour; set aside.

6. Line the pie shell with foil and fill it with pie weights or dried beans. Brush the pie border with the egg-yolk mixture and bake for 10 minutes. Remove the pie shell from the oven and reduce the oven temperature to 375°.

7. Remove the foil and weights from the pie shell and spoon the filling into the shell. Return the pie to the oven and bake it for another 20 minutes, or until the crust is golden; set aside to cool slightly.

8. In a small saucepan, warm the marmalade over low heat until it is pourable. Spoon the warmed marmalade over the pie filling.

COCONUT CREAM PIE
WITH CHOCOLATE CRUST

SERVES 6 TO 8

ONE 7-OUNCE PACKAGE SHREDDED
    COCONUT
3 OUNCES SEMISWEET CHOCOLATE
2 TABLESPOONS BUTTER
⅓ CUP GRANULATED SUGAR
¼ CUP CORNSTARCH

4 EGG YOLKS
2 CUPS MILK
½ TEASPOON COCONUT EXTRACT
½ CUP HEAVY CREAM
2 TABLESPOONS POWDERED SUGAR

1. Preheat the oven to 325°.

2. Spread the coconut on a baking sheet and toast it in the oven, stirring occasionally, until lightly browned, about 10 minutes.

3. Meanwhile, in the top of a double boiler over hot, not simmering, water, melt the chocolate and butter. Remove the pan from the heat and stir in 2 cups of the coconut.

4. Turn the coconut-chocolate mixture into a 9-inch pie pan and pat it evenly into the pan to form a crust. Cover the crust with plastic wrap and refrigerate it for at least 15 minutes, or until firm.

5. Meanwhile, in a medium saucepan, combine the granulated sugar and cornstarch. Gradually whisk in the egg yolks, then slowly add the milk, whisking constantly, until the

mixture is smooth and the sugar is dissolved. Place the pan over medium heat, and cook the mixture, whisking constantly, until it is thick enough to coat the back of a spoon, 5 to 10 minutes. Remove the pan from the heat.

6. Stir in the coconut extract and ¾ cup of the remaining toasted coconut. Let the filling cool slightly, then place a circle of wax paper directly on the surface of the custard to prevent a skin from forming. Place the filling in the refrigerator to chill for at least 1 hour.

7. Just before serving, in a medium bowl, whip the cream with the powdered sugar until stiff.

8. Spoon the filling into the crust. Top the pie with the whipped cream, then sprinkle with the remaining ¼ cup coconut.

GRASSHOPPER PIE

SERVES 6 TO 8

ONE 8½-OUNCE PACKAGE CHOCOLATE
  WAFERS
⅓ CUP BUTTER, MELTED
1 CUP LIGHT CREAM OR HALF-AND-
  HALF
4½ CUPS MARSHMALLOWS

¼ CUP GREEN CRÈME DE MENTHE
¼ CUP CRÈME DE CACAO
2½ CUPS HEAVY CREAM
2 TABLESPOONS POWDERED SUGAR
CHOCOLATE SHAVINGS, FOR GARNISH
  (OPTIONAL)

1. Place the wafers in a food processor or blender and process to form fine crumbs. Turn the crumbs into a bowl, add the melted butter, and blend well. Press the crumb mixture evenly into a 9-inch pie pan to form a crust; set aside.

2. In a medium saucepan, combine the light cream and marshmallows, and cook over medium heat, stirring constantly, until the marshmallows are completely melted, about 5 minutes. Remove the pan from the heat and stir in the crème de menthe and crème de cacao. Cover the pan and set the filling aside to cool to room temperature.

3. When the filling is cool, in a large bowl, beat 1½ cups of the heavy cream until stiff. Stir ¼ of the whipped cream into the filling. Fold in the remaining whipped cream, then turn the filling into the crust, spreading it evenly. Place the pie in the freezer for at least 6 hours, or overnight.

4. Allow the pie to stand at room temperature for 15 minutes before serving.

5. Meanwhile, whip the remaining 1 cup heavy cream with the powdered sugar until stiff. Top the pie with the whipped cream and sprinkle with chocolate shavings, if desired.

SUBSTITUTION: *This recipe calls for 2 types of liqueur: chocolate-flavored crème de cacao and minty green crème de menthe. If you wish, omit the crème de cacao and use a total of ½ cup of crème de menthe instead. If you do use the chocolate liqueur, be sure to buy the white (clear) type, and not the dark brown variety.*

Fudge Pie with Gingersnap Crust

SERVES 6 TO 8

35 GINGERSNAPS

2 STICKS BUTTER

2 TABLESPOONS GRANULATED SUGAR

6 OUNCES UNSWEETENED CHOCOLATE

4 EGGS

¾ CUP BROWN SUGAR

⅔ CUP HEAVY CREAM

1 TEASPOON VANILLA EXTRACT

LIGHTLY SWEETENED WHIPPED CREAM
   AND CHOCOLATE CURLS, FOR
   GARNISH (OPTIONAL)

1. Preheat the oven to 325°.

2. Place the gingersnaps in a food processor or blender and process to form fine crumbs. Turn the crumbs into a bowl. Melt 1 stick of the butter and add it and the granulated sugar to the bowl and blend well. Press the crumb mixture evenly into a 9-inch pie pan to form a crust; set aside.

3. In a small saucepan, melt the chocolate and the remaining butter over very low heat, stirring until smooth. Remove the pan from the heat and set aside to cool.

4. In a large bowl, beat the eggs. Beat in the brown sugar, then beat in the cooled chocolate mixture. Beat in the heavy cream and vanilla. Pour the filling into the crust and bake for 25 to 30 minutes, or until the filling is just set. The center may still be slightly wobbly.

5. Let the pie cool to room temperature, then slice it into wedges and top each serving with whipped cream and chocolate curls, if desired.

KITCHEN NOTE: *Chocolate curls make a splendid topping for any chocolate dessert. To make them, you'll need a thick chocolate bar or a good-sized chunk of chocolate, at room temperature. Hold the chocolate in the palm of your hand and slowly draw a swivel-bladed vegetable peeler over the surface (or along the edge).*

Maple Custard Pie

SERVES 6 TO 8

1½ CUPS FLOUR
¼ TEASPOON SALT
1 TABLESPOON GRANULATED SUGAR
6 TABLESPOONS UNSALTED BUTTER, AT
    ROOM TEMPERATURE
2 TABLESPOONS VEGETABLE
    SHORTENING

3 TO 4 TABLESPOONS ICE WATER
1 CUP HEAVY CREAM
1 CUP MILK
½ CUP MAPLE SYRUP
1 TEASPOON VANILLA EXTRACT
4 EGGS

1. Preheat the oven to 400°. In a large bowl, combine the flour, salt, and sugar. With a pastry blender or 2 knives, cut the unsalted butter and the shortening into the flour until it resembles coarse crumbs. Pour 3 tablespoons of ice water over the mixture all at once, toss together lightly, and gather the dough into a ball. If the dough crumbles, add up to 1 tablespoon more ice water by drops until the particles adhere.

2. On a lightly floured surface, roll the dough into a 12-inch circle. Fit the dough into a 9-inch pie pan. Trim the overhang to an even 1 inch and fold the dough under; crimp the dough to form a decorative border. Prick the pastry with a fork. Line the pie shell with foil, fill it with pie weights or dried beans, and bake for 10 minutes. Remove the crust from the oven and reduce the temperature to 325°.

3. In a small saucepan, warm the cream, milk, maple syrup, and vanilla over medium heat, stirring occasionally, until small bubbles appear around the edges of the pan. Remove the pan from the heat and cover to keep warm.

4. In a medium bowl, beat the eggs for 2 to 3 minutes until they begin to thicken and cling to the beater. Beating constantly, pour in the maple mixture in a slow, thin stream. Pour the filling into the pie shell. Bake for 40 minutes, or until a knife inserted into the center of the pie comes out clean. Remove the pie from the oven and let it cool to room temperature before serving.

Bourbon-Pecan Pie

SERVES 6 TO 8

1¼ CUPS FLOUR

¾ TEASPOON SALT

1 STICK BUTTER, AT ROOM
  TEMPERATURE

3 TABLESPOONS VEGETABLE
  SHORTENING

4 TO 5 TABLESPOONS ICE WATER

⅓ CUP DARK BROWN SUGAR

3 EGGS

¾ CUP DARK CORN SYRUP

2 TABLESPOONS BOURBON

1½ CUPS PECAN HALVES

1. In a large bowl, combine the flour and salt. With a pastry blender or 2 knives, cut in 4 tablespoons of butter and the shortening until the mixture resembles coarse crumbs. Sprinkle 4 tablespoons of the ice water over the mixture and toss it with a fork. The dough should be moistened just enough so that it holds together when it is formed into a ball. If necessary, add up to 1 tablespoon more ice water, drop by drop. Shape the dough into a flat disc, wrap in plastic wrap, and refrigerate for at least 30 minutes, or until well chilled.

2. On a lightly floured surface, roll the dough out to a 12-inch circle. Fit the dough into a 9-inch pie pan. Trim the overhang to an even ½ inch and fold it under; crimp the dough to form a decorative border. Prick the pastry with a fork. Place the pie shell in the freezer for at least 15 minutes before filling and baking.

3. Preheat the oven to 350°.

4. In a mixing bowl, cream the remaining 4 tablespoons butter and the sugar. Add the eggs, 1 at a time, blending well after each addition. Beat in the corn syrup and bourbon until well blended. Stir in the pecans.

5. Pour the mixture into the pie shell and bake for 40 to 45 minutes, or until the filling has set and is slightly puffed. Cool the pie on a rack before serving.

KITCHEN NOTE: *Pecan pies sometimes have a tendency to over-brown. Baking the pie on a slightly lower oven rack, rather than in the center of the oven, will help prevent this from happening.*

CRANBERRY CHIFFON PIE

SERVES 6 TO 8

2 CUPS GROUND PECANS
¾ CUP PLUS 7 TABLESPOONS SUGAR
4 TABLESPOONS BUTTER, MELTED
2 CUPS CRANBERRY JUICE
1 ENVELOPE UNFLAVORED GELATIN
¾ CUP CRANBERRIES

3 EGG WHITES
½ TEASPOON SALT
½ CUP HEAVY CREAM, CHILLED
2 CUPS SWEETENED WHIPPED CREAM
14 PECAN HALVES

1. Preheat the oven to 350°. In a large bowl, combine the ground pecans and 7 tablespoons of sugar. Sprinkle the melted butter over them and stir until the butter is completely absorbed. Scatter the mixture into a 9-inch pie pan. Press the crust firmly and evenly against the bottom and sides of the pan. Bake for 10 minutes, or until the crust browns lightly and is firm to the touch. Let the crust cool to room temperature.

2. Meanwhile, pour ¼ cup of the cranberry juice into a heatproof measuring cup and sprinkle it with the gelatin. When the gelatin has softened for 2 to 3 minutes, set the cup in a small skillet of simmering water and cook over low heat, stirring constantly, until the gelatin dissolves. Remove the skillet from the heat but leave the cup in the water to keep the gelatin fluid and warm.

3. In a small saucepan, combine the cranberries, the remaining 1¾ cups of cranberry juice, and ½ cup of sugar and bring to a boil over high heat, stirring constantly until the sugar dissolves. Reduce the heat to low and simmer, uncovered, for 4 to 5 minutes, stirring occasionally, until the berries are tender. Remove the pan from the heat, add the gelatin, and stir until dissolved. Reserving the liquid, drain and chop the cranberries.

4. Meanwhile, in a large bowl, beat the egg whites and salt until frothy. Beat in the remaining ¼ cup of sugar until stiff peaks form. In another large bowl, whip the cream until stiff peaks form. Gently fold the egg-white mixture into the cream.

5. Pour the egg-white-and-cream mixture over the thickened cranberry syrup and fold in until no trace of white remains. Gently fold in the chopped cranberries. Pour the mixture into the pie crust and refrigerate for at least 3 hours, or until the chiffon is firm. Just before serving, spread the whipped cream over the entire surface of the pie. Arrange the pecan halves decoratively on top.

CIDER PIE

SERVES 6 TO 8

1½ CUPS FLOUR

½ TEASPOON SALT

1 TABLESPOON GRANULATED SUGAR

6 TABLESPOONS UNSALTED BUTTER, AT
ROOM TEMPERATURE

2 TABLESPOONS VEGETABLE
SHORTENING

3 TO 4 TABLESPOONS ICE WATER

1½ CUPS APPLE CIDER

1 CUP DARK BROWN SUGAR

2 TABLESPOONS BUTTER, CUT INTO
PIECES

3 EGG YOLKS

2 EGG WHITES

⅛ TEASPOON GROUND NUTMEG

1. Preheat the oven to 400°. In a large bowl, combine the flour, ¼ teaspoon salt, and the sugar. With a pastry blender or 2 knives, cut the unsalted butter and the shortening into the flour until it resembles coarse crumbs. Pour 3 tablespoons of ice water over the mixture all at once, toss together lightly, and gather the dough into a ball. If the dough crumbles, add up to 1 tablespoon more ice water by drops until the particles adhere.

2. On a lightly floured surface, roll the dough into a 12-inch circle. Fit the dough into a 9-inch pie pan. Trim the overhang to an even 1 inch and fold the dough under; crimp the dough to form a decorative border. Prick the pastry with a fork. Line the pie shell with foil, fill it with pie weights or dried beans, and bake for 10 minutes. Remove the crust from the oven and reduce the temperature to 350°.

3. In a medium saucepan, boil the cider, uncovered, over high heat until it is reduced to ¾ cup. Add the brown sugar, butter pieces, and ¼ teaspoon salt, and stir until the sugar dissolves and the butter melts. Remove from the heat.

4. In a small bowl, lightly beat the egg yolks. Stir in 2 tablespoons of the cider mixture, then gradually pour the yolks into the cider, whisking all the while.

5. In a large bowl, beat the egg whites until stiff peaks form. Scoop the egg whites over the cider mixture and beat them together gently but thoroughly with a whisk.

6. Pour the mixture into the pie shell and sprinkle the top with the nutmeg. Bake for 30 minutes, or until a knife inserted into the center of the pie comes out clean. Cool to room temperature before serving.

⊙sgood Pie

SERVES 6 TO 8

1¼ CUPS PLUS 1 TABLESPOON FLOUR

¼ TEASPOON SALT

6 TABLESPOONS BUTTER—4 AT ROOM
  TEMPERATURE, 2 MELTED

3 TABLESPOONS VEGETABLE
  SHORTENING

4 TO 5 TABLESPOONS ICE WATER

1 CUP CHOPPED PECANS

1 CUP DRIED APRICOTS, CHOPPED

1 CUP RAISINS

½ TEASPOON ALLSPICE

½ TEASPOON CINNAMON

½ TEASPOON NUTMEG

3 EGGS, SEPARATED

½ CUP SUGAR

2 TABLESPOONS CIDER VINEGAR

1. Preheat the oven to 400°. In a large bowl, combine 1¼ cups of the flour and the salt. With a pastry blender or 2 knives, cut in the 4 tablespoons of room temperature butter and the shortening until the mixture resembles coarse crumbs. Sprinkle 4 tablespoons of the ice water over the mixture and toss it with a fork. The dough should be moistened enough so that it holds together when it is formed into a ball. If necessary, add up to 1 tablespoon more ice water, drop by drop.

2. On a lightly floured surface, roll the dough into a 12-inch circle. Fit the dough into a 9-inch pie pan. Trim the overhang to an even ½ inch and fold the dough under; crimp the dough to form a decorative border. Prick the pastry with a fork. Line the pie shell with foil, fill it with pie weights or dried beans, and bake it for 10 minutes. Remove the foil and weights and set the pie shell aside to cool; reduce the oven temperature to 375°.

3. In a large bowl, combine the pecans, apricots, raisins, allspice, cinnamon, nutmeg, and the remaining tablespoon flour, and toss to coat; set aside.

4. In a large bowl, beat the egg yolks and sugar until thick and light-colored. Add the melted butter and the vinegar, and stir to blend. Stir in the nut-fruit mixture.

5. In another large bowl, beat the egg whites until stiff but not dry. Gently fold the beaten whites into the nut-fruit mixture.

6. Spread the filling evenly in the pie shell and bake for 18 to 20 minutes, or until the filling is set and golden, and a knife inserted into the center of the pie comes out clean.

KITCHEN NOTE: *Folklore has it that this pie's name arises from the fact that it's "oh, so good!" Taste the pie, and you'll likely agree.*

Pumpkin Pie

SERVES 6 TO 8

1¼ CUPS FLOUR

¼ TEASPOON SALT

4 TABLESPOONS VEGETABLE SHORTENING

2 TABLESPOONS BUTTER, AT ROOM TEMPERATURE

3 TABLESPOONS ICE WATER

½ CUP HEAVY CREAM

½ CUP MILK

¾ CUP DARK BROWN SUGAR

1 TEASPOON CINNAMON

⅛ TEASPOON CLOVES

½ TEASPOON GROUND GINGER

5 EGGS, LIGHTLY BEATEN

1½ CUPS CANNED PUMPKIN

1. Preheat the oven to 350°.

2. In a large bowl, combine the flour and salt. With a pastry blender or 2 knives, cut the shortening and butter into the flour until it resembles coarse crumbs. Pour the ice water over the mixture, toss together, and press and knead gently with your hands until the dough can be gathered into a compact ball.

3. On a lightly floured surface, roll the dough out to a 12-inch circle. Fit the dough into a 9-inch pie pan. Trim the overhang to an even ½ inch and fold it under; crimp the dough to form a decorative border. Prick the pastry with a fork.

4. In a large bowl, combine the cream, milk, brown sugar, cinnamon, cloves, and ginger. Add the eggs and pumpkin and stir until well blended. Carefully pour the filling into the pie shell. Bake for 40 to 50 minutes in the center of the oven until the filling is firm and the center of the pie barely quivers when the pie pan is gently moved back and forth. Serve warm or at room temperature.

Sweet Potato Pie

SERVES 6 TO 8

1½ CUPS FLOUR

½ TEASPOON SALT

6 TABLESPOONS UNSALTED BUTTER, AT ROOM TEMPERATURE

2 TABLESPOONS VEGETABLE SHORTENING

3 TO 4 TABLESPOONS ICE WATER

4 MEDIUM SWEET POTATOES, PEELED AND QUARTERED

¾ CUP DARK BROWN SUGAR

4 TABLESPOONS BUTTER, AT ROOM TEMPERATURE

3 EGGS

⅓ CUP LIGHT CORN SYRUP

⅓ CUP MILK

2 TEASPOONS GRATED LEMON ZEST

1 TEASPOON VANILLA EXTRACT

¼ TEASPOON NUTMEG

1. Preheat the oven to 400°. In a large bowl, combine the flour and ¼ teaspoon of salt. With a pastry blender or 2 knives, cut the unsalted butter and the shortening into the flour until it resembles coarse crumbs. Pour 3 tablespoons of ice water over the mixture all at once, toss together lightly, and gather the dough into a ball. If the dough crumbles, add up to 1 tablespoon more ice water by drops until the particles adhere.

2. On a lightly floured surface, roll the dough into a 12-inch circle. Fit the dough into a 9-inch pie pan. Trim the overhang to an even 1 inch and fold the dough under; crimp the dough to form a decorative border. Prick the pastry with a fork. Line the pie shell with foil, fill it with pie weights or dried beans, and bake for 10 minutes. Remove the crust from the oven and reduce the oven temperature to 325°.

3. In a large pot of water, boil the sweet potatoes until tender; drain. In a food processor or blender, purée the sweet potatoes.

4. In a large bowl, cream the sugar and the 4 tablespoons butter until light and fluffy. Beat in the sweet potatoes until well blended. Add the eggs, 1 at a time, beating well after each addition. Beat in the corn syrup, milk, lemon zest, vanilla, nutmeg, and remaining ¼ teaspoon salt until smooth.

5. Pour the sweet potato filling into the pie shell. Bake for 35 minutes, or until a knife inserted into the center comes out clean.

CLASSIC APPLE PIE

SERVES 6 TO 8

2½ CUPS PLUS 1 TABLESPOON FLOUR
¼ TEASPOON SALT
8 TABLESPOONS VEGETABLE
   SHORTENING
6 TABLESPOONS BUTTER, AT ROOM
   TEMPERATURE
6 TABLESPOONS ICE WATER

¾ CUP SUGAR
1 TEASPOON CINNAMON
¼ TEASPOON ALLSPICE
¼ TEASPOON NUTMEG
6 CUPS PEELED AND SLICED BAKING
   APPLES
1 TABLESPOON FRESH LEMON JUICE

1. Preheat the oven to 375°.

2. In a large bowl, combine 2½ cups of the flour and the salt. With a pastry blender or 2 knives, cut the shortening and 4 tablespoons of butter into the flour until it resembles coarse crumbs. Pour the ice water over the mixture, toss together, and press and knead gently with your hands until the dough can be gathered into a compact ball. Divide the dough into 2 equal portions.

3. On a lightly floured surface, roll 1 portion of the dough into a 12-inch circle. Fit the dough into a 9-inch pie pan. Trim the overhang so that the pastry is even with the outer rim of the pie pan.

4. In a large bowl, combine the sugar, cinnamon, allspice, nutmeg, and the remaining tablespoon of flour. Add the apples and the lemon juice, and toss together gently but thoroughly. Fill the pie shell with the apple mixture, mounding it somewhat higher in the center. Dot the top of the filling with the remaining 2 tablespoons of butter.

5. Roll out the remaining portion of dough into a 12-inch circle. Drape the crust gently over the filling. Tuck the overhanging dough under the edge of the bottom crust all around the rim and then press down with the tines of a fork to seal the 2 crusts securely. Cut several steam vents in the top crust. Bake for 40 minutes, or until the crust is golden brown. Serve warm or at room temperature.

SOUR CHERRY PIE

SERVES 6 TO 8

2½ CUPS FLOUR
¼ TEASPOON SALT
8 TABLESPOONS VEGETABLE
   SHORTENING
7 TABLESPOONS BUTTER, AT ROOM
   TEMPERATURE

6 TABLESPOONS ICE WATER
6 CUPS PITTED SOUR CHERRIES
¼ CUP QUICK-COOKING TAPIOCA
1 CUP SUGAR
1½ TABLESPOONS FRESH LEMON JUICE
¼ TEASPOON ALMOND EXTRACT

1. In a large bowl, combine the flour and salt. With a pastry blender or 2 knives, cut the shortening and 6 tablespoons of butter into the flour until it resembles coarse crumbs. Pour the ice water over the mixture, toss together, and press and knead gently with your hands until the dough can be gathered into a compact ball. Divide the dough into 2 equal portions.

2. On a lightly floured surface, roll 1 portion of the dough into a 12-inch circle. Fit the dough into a 9-inch pie pan. Trim the overhang so that the pastry is even with the outer rim of the pie pan.

3. In a large bowl, combine the cherries, tapioca, sugar, lemon juice, and almond extract and toss together gently but thoroughly. Let the mixture rest uncovered at room temperature for about 10 minutes. Spoon the filling into the pie shell and dot with the remaining tablespoon of butter.

4. Preheat the oven to 450°. Roll out the remaining portion of dough into a 12-inch circle. Drape the crust gently over the filling. Tuck the overhanging dough under the edge of the bottom crust all around the rim and then press down with the tines of a fork to seal the 2 crusts securely. Cut several steam vents in the top crust. Bake for 10 minutes, then lower the oven temperature to 350° and bake another 40 to 45 minutes, or until the top is golden brown.

PEAR-WALNUT PIE

SERVES 6 TO 8

3 CUPS PLUS 1 TABLESPOON FLOUR
½ TEASPOON SALT
1 CUP PLUS 2 TABLESPOONS SUGAR
1½ STICKS UNSALTED BUTTER, AT
    ROOM TEMPERATURE
4 TABLESPOONS VEGETABLE
    SHORTENING

6 TO 8 TABLESPOONS ICE WATER
4 CUPS PEELED AND SLICED PEARS
⅓ CUP COARSELY CHOPPED WALNUTS
½ CUP RAISINS
¼ CUP FRESH ORANGE JUICE
1 TEASPOON GRATED ORANGE ZEST
3 TABLESPOONS BUTTER, MELTED

1. In a large bowl, combine 3 cups of flour, the salt, and 2 tablespoons of sugar. With a pastry blender or 2 knives, cut the unsalted butter and vegetable shortening into the flour until it resembles coarse crumbs. Pour 6 tablespoons of ice water over the mixture all at once, toss together lightly, and gather the dough into a ball. If the dough crumbles, add up to 2 tablespoons more ice water by drops until the particles adhere. Divide the dough into 2 equal portions.

2. On a lightly floured surface, roll 1 portion of the dough into a 12-inch circle. Fit the dough into a 9-inch pie pan. Trim the overhang so that the pastry is even with the outer rim of the pie pan.

3. In a large bowl, stir together the pears, walnuts, 1 cup sugar, 1 tablespoon of flour, the raisins, orange juice, orange zest, and the melted butter. Spoon the filling into the pie shell.

4. Preheat the oven to 400°. Roll out the remaining portion of dough into a 12-inch circle, then cut it into ½-inch-wide strips. Place the strips on top of the pie in a lattice pattern. With a pastry brush dipped in cold water, lightly moisten the ends of the strips at the point where they meet the bottom pastry shell. Trim the excess off the strips and crimp them firmly in place with your fingers or the tines of a fork.

5. Bake the pie for about 1 hour, or until the pastry is golden brown. If the edge of the pie begins to brown too quickly, cover it loosely with a strip of foil. Let the pie cool to room temperature before serving.

LEMON CHESS PIE

SERVES 6 TO 8

1¼ CUPS FLOUR

¼ TEASPOON SALT

1 STICK BUTTER, AT ROOM
   TEMPERATURE

3 TABLESPOONS VEGETABLE
   SHORTENING

4 TO 5 TABLESPOONS ICE WATER

¾ CUP SUGAR

2 TABLESPOONS CORNMEAL

5 EGGS

1 TABLESPOON GRATED LEMON ZEST

¼ CUP FRESH LEMON JUICE

1. Preheat the oven to 325°.

2. In a large bowl, combine the flour and salt. With a pastry blender or 2 knives, cut 4 tablespoons of butter and the shortening into the flour until the mixture resembles coarse crumbs. Sprinkle 4 tablespoons of the ice water over the mixture and toss it with a fork. The dough should be moistened just enough so that it holds together when it is formed into a ball. If necessary, add up to 1 table-spoon more ice water, drop by drop.

3. On a lightly floured surface, roll the dough into a 12-inch circle. Fit the dough into a 9-inch pie pan. Trim the overhang to an even ½ inch and fold the dough under; crimp the dough to form a decorative border. Prick the pastry with a fork.

4. In a medium bowl, cream the remaining 4 tablespoons butter and the sugar. Beat in the cornmeal. Add the eggs, 1 at a time, beating well after each addition. Beat in the lemon zest and lemon juice.

5. Pour the filling into the pie shell and bake for 45 minutes, or until a knife inserted into the center of the pie comes out clean. Cool the pie on a rack.

VARIATION: *Use light brown sugar instead of granulated sugar for a slightly darker, richer-tasting pie with a hint of butterscotch.*

Plum Pudding

SERVES 4

1½ CUPS DRIED CURRANTS

2 CUPS DARK RAISINS

2 CUPS GOLDEN RAISINS

¾ CUP FINELY CHOPPED CANDIED
   MIXED FRUIT PEEL

¾ CUP CHOPPED CANDIED CHERRIES

1 CUP SLIVERED ALMONDS

1 MEDIUM APPLE, PEELED AND
   COARSELY CHOPPED

1 SMALL CARROT, COARSELY CHOPPED

2 TABLESPOONS GRATED ORANGE ZEST

2 TEASPOONS GRATED LEMON ZEST

½ POUND FINELY CHOPPED BEEF SUET

2 CUPS FLOUR

4 CUPS FRESH BREAD CRUMBS

1 CUP DARK BROWN SUGAR

1 TEASPOON ALLSPICE

1 TEASPOON SALT

6 EGGS

1 CUP BRANDY

⅓ CUP FRESH ORANGE JUICE

¼ CUP FRESH LEMON JUICE

I. In a large bowl, combine the currants, dark raisins, golden raisins, candied fruit peel, cherries, almonds, apple, carrot, orange and lemon zests, and beef suet, tossing until well mixed. Stir in the flour, bread crumbs, brown sugar, allspice, and salt.

2. In another large bowl, beat the eggs until frothy. Stir in the brandy, orange juice, and lemon juice, and pour over the fruit mixture. Knead vigorously with both hands, then beat with a wooden spoon until blended. Drape a dampened kitchen towel over the bowl and refrigerate for at least 12 hours.

3. Spoon the mixture into four 1-quart molds. Cover each mold securely with a strip of buttered foil. Place the molds in a large pot and pour in enough boiling water to come

about ¾ of the way up their sides. Bring to a boil, cover the pot tightly, reduce the heat to low and steam the puddings for 8 hours. Add additional water as necessary.

4. Remove the puddings from the water and let cool to room temperature. Refrigerate for at least 24 hours before serving.

5. To serve, place the mold in a pot and pour in enough boiling water to come about ¾ of the way up the sides of the mold. Bring to a boil, reduce the heat to low and steam, covered, for 1 hour. Run a knife around the inside edges of the mold and place an inverted serving plate over it. Grasping the mold and plate firmly together, turn them over. The pudding should slide out easily.

Steamed Cranberry Pudding

SERVES 6 TO 8

1½ STICKS BUTTER, AT ROOM
    TEMPERATURE
½ CUP DARK BROWN SUGAR
1 EGG, LIGHTLY BEATEN
1 TEASPOON ORANGE EXTRACT
3 TEASPOONS GRATED ORANGE ZEST
1 CUP FLOUR
¼ CUP FRESH BREAD CRUMBS

2 TEASPOONS BAKING POWDER
½ TEASPOON SALT
⅔ CUP MILK
2 CUPS FRESH OR FROZEN CRANBERRIES
1 CUP MIXED DRIED FRUIT, CHOPPED
½ CUP CHOPPED WALNUTS
¾ CUP POWDERED SUGAR
2 TABLESPOONS HEAVY CREAM

1. In a medium bowl, cream 1 stick of the butter and the brown sugar. Beat in the egg, ½ teaspoon orange extract, and 2 teaspoons orange zest. In a small bowl, combine the flour, bread crumbs, baking powder, and salt.

2. Alternating between the 2, beat the dry ingredients and the milk into the butter mixture. In a large bowl, combine the cranberries, dried fruit, and walnuts. Fold the fruit-nut mixture into the batter.

3. Spread the batter evenly in a 1½-quart soufflé dish. Rap the dish lightly once or twice on the counter to remove any air pockets. Cover the dish tightly with foil and tie the foil in place with string. Place the dish on a rack set in a large, deep pot with a cover. Pour in 1 inch of boiling water. Cover the pot and steam the pudding over low heat until firm, about 2 hours, adding more boiling water as necessary.

4. Meanwhile, in a medium bowl, cream the remaining 4 tablespoons butter and the powdered sugar. Beat in the heavy cream, and the remaining orange extract and zest. Refrigerate the hard sauce until serving time.

5. Let the pudding cool slightly in the dish for about 10 minutes. Then serve warm with the hard sauce.

ENGLISH TRIFLE

SERVES 6 TO 8

¼ CUP CANDIED CHERRIES
¼ CUP CANDIED ANGELICA, CUT INTO
   1-INCH STRIPS
⅓ CUP RAISINS
18 LADYFINGERS

¼ CUP MADEIRA
3 EGGS
3 TABLESPOONS SUGAR
1 CUP MILK
½ CUP HEAVY CREAM

1. Generously grease the sides and bottom of a 1½-quart mold with cold butter.

2. Slice a cherry in half, place it, cut-side up, in the center of the mold, and arrange 8 strips of the angelica in a spokelike pattern around it. Decorate the sides of the basin with 6 to 8 rows of raisins, arranging them so that the rows reach about 4 inches up the sides of the mold. Split 9 ladyfingers in half, and place 3 or 4 of the halves, cut-side up, on the bottom of the mold. Sprinkle with 2 tablespoons of the Madeira. Stand 14 or 15 ladyfinger halves, cut-side in, around the inside of the mold, overlapping them slightly to line the sides.

3. Cut the remaining angelica and cherries into ¼-inch dice and combine them with the remaining raisins in a small bowl. Stir in 1 tablespoon of Madeira and set aside.

4. In a medium bowl, beat the eggs, sugar, milk, and cream until thick.

5. Sprinkle the bottom layer of ladyfingers with ⅓ of the diced fruit, pour on ⅓ of the custard mixture, and sprinkle with 2 crumbled ladyfingers. Repeat this process 2 times, then sprinkle with the remaining Madeira.

6. Cover each mold securely with a strip of buttered foil. Place the pudding in a large pot and pour in enough boiling water to come ¾ of the way up the sides of the mold. Bring to a boil over high heat, cover the pot tightly, reduce the heat to low, and steam for 1¼ hours. Replenish the water as necessary.

7. Let the pudding rest for 2 to 3 minutes. Place an inverted plate over the top, grasp the edges of the mold and plate together firmly, and turn them over quickly. The pudding should slide out easily. If any raisins or bits of fruit cling to the mold, return them to their original position on the pudding. Serve the pudding warm.

Fruit-Filled Bread Pudding

SERVES 6 TO 8

2 QUARTS FRESH OR FROZEN THAWED
   RASPBERRIES, BLACKBERRIES,
   BLUEBERRIES, OR RED CURRANTS
1¼ CUPS SUGAR

10 TO 12 SLICES HOMEMADE-TYPE
   WHITE BREAD
1 CUP HEAVY CREAM

1. Place the berries in a large bowl, sprinkle with the sugar, and toss until the sugar is dissolved. Set aside.

2. Cut 1 slice of bread into a circle so that it will exactly fit the bottom of a 2-quart mold, and set it in place. Trim 6 or 7 slices of the bread into truncated wedge shapes 4 inches wide across the top and 3 inches wide across the bottom. Stand the wedges, narrow-end down, around the inner surface of the mold, overlapping them by about ¼ inch. Ladle the fruit mixture into the mold, and cover the top completely with the remaining bread. Cover the top of the mold with a flat plate, and on it set a 3- to 4-pound kitchen weight, or a heavy pan or casserole. Refrigerate the pudding for at least 12 hours, until the bread is completely saturated with the fruit syrup.

3. To remove the pudding from the mold, place a chilled serving plate upside down over it and, grasping the plate and mold firmly together, quickly invert them. The pudding should slide out easily.

4. In a large chilled bowl, beat the cream until it holds its shape softly. Serve the whipped cream separately with the pudding.

KITCHEN NOTE: *The British call this delectable dessert "summer pudding," and it does capture the essence of berry season. To make the pudding easier to turn out, line the mold with plastic wrap, leaving a generous overhang around the top. A 2-quart saucepan or bowl will serve perfectly well if you don't have a pudding mold.*

Sweet Pudding with Nuts and Candied Fruits

SERVES 8 TO 10

1 QUART MILK
½ CUP SUGAR
¾ CUP SEMOLINA OR FARINA
½ TEASPOON ALMOND EXTRACT
½ CUP GROUND WALNUTS OR PECANS
½ CUP GROUND ALMONDS

1 CUP APRICOT PRESERVES
2 TABLESPOONS COLD WATER
1 CUP FINELY CHOPPED MIXED
   CANDIED FRUITS
½ CUP VANILLA WAFER CRUMBS

1. Preheat the oven to 350°. Grease the bottom and sides of an 8-inch springform pan.

2. In a medium saucepan, combine the milk and sugar and bring to a boil over medium heat. Stirring constantly, slowly pour in the semolina, lower the heat, and simmer, uncovered, for about 5 minutes, or until the mixture thickens. Remove from the heat and stir in the almond extract, walnuts, and almonds.

3. In a small saucepan, combine the apricot preserves and water. Stirring constantly, cook over medium heat for 1 to 2 minutes, then rub through a fine sieve set over a bowl. Stir in the candied fruits.

4. Spread ⅓ of the semolina mixture into the prepared pan. Spread with half the fruit and jam, then make another layer, using half the remaining semolina. Spread the remaining fruit and jam on top and cover with the remaining semolina. Sprinkle the vanilla wafer crumbs evenly over the top.

5. Bake for 30 minutes, or until the top is golden brown. Cool to room temperature. Remove the springform and refrigerate until ready to serve.

CARAMEL CUSTARDS WITH WARM APRICOT COMPOTE

SERVES 4

¼ CUP LIGHT BROWN SUGAR	¼ POUND DRIED APRICOTS
4 EGGS	1 CUP CRANBERRY JUICE
3 TABLESPOONS MAPLE SYRUP	½ TEASPOON GRATED LEMON ZEST
1½ CUPS HEAVY CREAM	½ CUP FRESH OR FROZEN CRANBERRIES
½ TEASPOON VANILLA EXTRACT	1 TABLESPOON DARK RUM

1. Place 1 tablespoon of the brown sugar in the bottom of each of 4 individual soufflé dishes or 6-ounce custard cups. Spread the sugar into a smooth, even layer; set aside.

2. Preheat the oven to 350°.

3. In a large bowl, beat the eggs until light. Stir in the maple syrup, cream, and vanilla, and continue beating until well blended. Divide the custard evenly among the prepared dishes. Set the dishes in a roasting pan placed on the middle rack of the oven. Pour hot water into the pan to reach halfway up the sides of the dishes.

4. Bake the custards for 35 to 40 minutes, or until they are firm and the tip of a knife inserted into the center comes out clean.

5. Meanwhile, in a medium saucepan, combine the apricots, cranberry juice, and lemon zest. Bring to a boil, then reduce the heat, cover the pan, and simmer until the apricots are very tender, about 20 minutes. Add the cranberries to the pan about 5 minutes before the apricots are done. Set the mixture aside, uncovered, to cool slightly.

6. With a potato masher, mash the apricots in the cooking liquid, leaving the fruit somewhat chunky. Stir in the rum, cover the pan, and set aside.

7. When the custards are done, remove them from the water and wipe the dishes dry. Immediately unmold the custards by running the tip of a knife around the edge of each dish, then carefully inverting the dish onto a dessert plate. Spoon some apricot compote over each custard and serve warm.

COCONUT RICE
PUDDING WITH RAISINS

SERVES 4 TO 6

1 CUP LONG-GRAIN WHITE RICE

4 CUPS MILK

1½ TEASPOONS CINNAMON

¼ TEASPOON GROUND CLOVES

¼ TEASPOON GROUND GINGER

2 CUPS SHREDDED COCONUT

¼ CUP SUGAR

1 TEASPOON SALT

½ CUP SEEDLESS RAISINS

NUTMEG

1. In a medium saucepan, bring 1 quart of water to a boil. Add the rice and cook, uncovered, for 5 minutes. Remove from the heat and drain.

2. In a large saucepan, combine the milk, cinnamon, cloves, ginger, coconut, sugar, and salt. Bring to a boil over high heat, then stir in the rice, cover the pan, and reduce the heat to low. Simmer for 30 minutes, stir in the raisins, and continue to cook, covered, for 10 minutes, or until the liquid is completely absorbed and the rice is tender.

3. Cool the pudding to room temperature and sprinkle with nutmeg before serving.

VARIATION: *This easy stove-top rice pudding is equally delicious made with currants or chopped dried figs.*

CANDY

MOLASSES TAFFY

MAKES 2 POUNDS

2 CUPS DARK MOLASSES
1 CUP GRANULATED SUGAR
½ CUP DARK BROWN SUGAR
¾ CUP WATER
4 TABLESPOONS BUTTER, CUT INTO
PIECES

2 TEASPOONS DISTILLED WHITE
VINEGAR
⅛ TEASPOON BAKING SODA
¼ TEASPOON SALT

1. Grease the bottom and sides of a large baking sheet.

2. In a large casserole, combine the molasses, granulated sugar, brown sugar, and water, and cook over high heat, stirring constantly until the molasses and sugar dissolve. Reduce the heat to moderate and boil, uncovered and undisturbed, until the syrup reaches 200° on a candy thermometer. Regulate the heat to prevent the syrup from foaming up and boiling over.

3. Stirring deeply and constantly with a wooden spoon to prevent the syrup from burning, continue to boil until it reaches a temperature of 250° on a candy thermometer, or until a few drops spooned into ice water immediately form a firm but still slightly pliable ball.

4. Remove the pan from the heat and beat in the butter, vinegar, baking soda, and salt. Pour the candy into the prepared pan and set it aside for about 10 minutes to cool slightly.

5. While the taffy is still warm and pliable, coat your hands with butter and pinch off about ¼ of the candy. Grasp the piece of candy with both hands and pull it into a ropelike strand about 1 inch thick. Fold the rope together into thirds and stretch it out again. Working quickly, repeat the pulling and folding until the taffy lightens to a pale brown color and begins to stiffen. Stretch the taffy into a rope and, with kitchen scissors, cut it into 1-inch lengths. Butter your hands again, pinch off another ¼ of the candy, and repeat the entire procedure until all the taffy has been pulled.

6. Serve at once, or wrap each piece of taffy in a 5-inch square of wax paper, twist the ends tightly, and store in a covered container.

PEANUT BRITTLE

MAKES 2 POUNDS

1½ CUPS SUGAR

⅓ CUP LIGHT CORN SYRUP

⅓ CUP COLD WATER

2 CUPS LIGHTLY SALTED TOASTED
  SPANISH PEANUTS, UNPEELED

2 TABLESPOONS UNSALTED BUTTER,
  CUT INTO PIECES

1 TEASPOON FRESH LEMON JUICE

1. Generously grease a baking sheet.

2. In a medium saucepan, combine the sugar, corn syrup, and water. Stirring constantly, cook over medium heat until the sugar dissolves. Increase the heat to high and bring the syrup to a boil. Continue to boil, uncovered, until the syrup reaches a temperature of 300° on a candy thermometer, meanwhile brushing down the crystals that form on the sides of the pan with a pastry brush lightly moistened with cold water.

3. Remove the pan from the heat and, with a wooden spoon, quickly stir in the nuts, butter, and lemon juice. Pour the mixture at once onto the prepared pan and set aside at room temperature for about 30 minutes, until the candy hardens. Break the peanut brittle into irregularly shaped pieces and serve at once, or wrap in plastic bags and store in a covered container.

VARIATION: *For coconut brittle, use 2 cups of shredded coconut in place of the peanuts. Cashew brittle is another delicious variation.*

ALMOND NOUGAT

MAKES 5 DOZEN

2½ CUPS GRANULATED SUGAR
1¾ CUPS LIGHT CORN SYRUP
3 EGG WHITES
⅓ CUP WATER
¾ CUP POWDERED SUGAR

2 TABLESPOONS BUTTER, CUT INTO
  PIECES
1 TEASPOON VANILLA EXTRACT
½ TEASPOON SALT
1½ CUPS COARSELY CHOPPED ALMONDS

1. Generously grease a large baking sheet.

2. Combine ½ cup of the granulated sugar and 1 cup of the corn syrup in a medium saucepan and stir over medium heat until the sugar dissolves. Raise the heat and boil briskly, uncovered and undisturbed, until the syrup reaches a temperature of 248° on a candy thermometer, or until a few drops spooned into ice water immediately form a firm but still slightly pliable ball.

3. Meanwhile, in a large bowl, beat the egg whites until stiff peaks form. Beating constantly, pour in the syrup in a slow, thin stream and continue to beat for 4 to 5 minutes, or until thickened. Let the candy mixture stand at room temperature while you prepare a second batch of syrup.

4. In a large saucepan, combine the remaining 2 cups of granulated sugar, the remaining ¾ cup of corn syrup, and the water, and stir over medium heat until the sugar dissolves. Increase the heat to high and boil briskly, un-

covered and undisturbed, until the syrup reaches a temperature of 272° on a candy thermometer, or until a drop spooned into ice water immediately separates into hard, but not brittle, threads. Watch the syrup carefully and adjust the heat when necessary.

5. Beating constantly at medium speed, pour the second batch of syrup into the egg-white-and-syrup mixture in a slow, thin stream. Continue to beat for about 10 minutes, or until the candy becomes opaque and creamy, then beat in the powdered sugar, butter, vanilla, and salt. With a wooden spoon, stir in the almonds.

6. Working quickly, spread the nougat mixture in the prepared pan. Pat it to a thickness of about ¾ inch with the palms of your hands and smooth the top with a rolling pin. When the nougat cools to room temperature, cover it with wax paper and set it aside in a cool place (not the refrigerator) for at least 12 hours. Cut the nougat into 1¼-inch squares.

Pecan Fudge

MAKES 2 DOZEN

6 TABLESPOONS BUTTER, CUT INTO
  PIECES
1 POUND POWDERED SUGAR
½ CUP COCOA POWDER

¼ CUP MILK
1 TABLESPOON VANILLA EXTRACT
¼ TEASPOON SALT
1 CUP CHOPPED PECANS

1. Grease the bottom and sides of an 8 x 8-inch baking pan.

2. In a medium saucepan, warm the butter and sugar over low heat until the butter is melted and the sugar is dissolved. Add the cocoa powder, milk, vanilla, and salt, and stir until smooth. Remove the pan from the heat and stir in the pecans.

3. Spread the mixture into the prepared pan. Let the fudge cool before cutting into squares.

Variations: *This fudge recipe is much less tricky than most because it's made with powdered sugar instead of granulated sugar. Like any fudge, it's open to lots of variations. You could use chopped crystallized ginger or shredded coconut instead of the pecans (if using coconut, replace the vanilla with almond extract). For peanut-butter fudge, substitute ¼ cup chunky peanut butter for the butter.*

Bourbon Balls

MAKES 5 DOZEN

8 OUNCES SEMISWEET CHOCOLATE,
  COARSELY CHOPPED
3 CUPS VANILLA WAFER CRUMBS
1 CUP FINELY CHOPPED PECANS

1⅔ CUPS SUGAR
½ CUP BOURBON
¼ CUP LIGHT CORN SYRUP

1. In a small skillet, melt the chocolate over very low heat, stirring almost constantly to prevent the bottom from scorching. Remove the pan from the heat and let the chocolate cool to lukewarm.

2. In a large bowl, combine the vanilla wafer crumbs, pecans, and ⅔ cup of sugar. Pour in the chocolate, bourbon, and corn syrup and stir vigorously with a wooden spoon until the ingredients are well combined.

3. To shape each bourbon ball, scoop up about a tablespoon of the mixture and pat it into a ball about 1 inch in diameter. Roll the balls in the remaining cup of sugar and, when they are lightly coated on all sides, place them in a widemouthed 1-quart jar equipped with a securely fitting lid. Cut 2 rounds from a double thickness of paper towels to fit inside the lid of the jar. Moisten the paper rounds with a little additional bourbon and press them tightly into the lid.

4. Seal the jar with the paper-lined lid and set the bourbon balls aside at room temperature for 3 to 4 days before serving.

KITCHEN NOTE: *When wines or liquors are used in cooking, most of the alcohol burns off. But these potent confections are not cooked, so they keep their "kick." Save them for the grown-ups!*

Pecan Pralines

MAKES 2 DOZEN

¼ CUP LIGHT CREAM OR EVAPORATED
    MILK
2 CUPS GRANULATED SUGAR
½ CUP WATER

⅓ CUP LIGHT BROWN SUGAR
⅛ TEASPOON SALT
1 TEASPOON VANILLA EXTRACT
2 CUPS COARSELY CHOPPED PECANS

1. Generously grease 2 large baking sheets.

2. In a small saucepan, warm the light cream over low heat. When bubbles begin to form around the edges of the pan, remove the pan from the heat and cover it tightly to keep warm.

3. Combine the granulated sugar and water in a medium skillet and bring to a boil over high heat, stirring until the sugar dissolves. Reduce the heat to medium and, gripping a pot holder in each hand, tip the pan back and forth gently until the syrup turns a rich, golden brown. This may take 10 minutes or more.

4. Remove the skillet from the heat and, with a wooden spoon, stir in the brown sugar and salt. Stirring constantly, pour in the warm cream in a slow, thin stream. Stir in the vanilla and the pecans.

5. To form each praline, ladle about 4 teaspoons of the pecan mixture onto the prepared baking sheet. As you proceed, space the pralines about 3 inches apart to allow room for them to spread into 2½-inch rounds. When the pralines have cooled to room temperature, transfer them to a serving plate.

WHITE CHOCOLATE TRUFFLES

MAKES 2 DOZEN

4 TABLESPOONS UNSALTED BUTTER, AT
    ROOM TEMPERATURE
2 CUPS POWDERED SUGAR

3 TABLESPOONS CHOCOLATE LIQUEUR
⅓ CUP FINELY CHOPPED PECANS
8 OUNCES WHITE CHOCOLATE

1. In a large bowl, cream the butter and sugar until light and fluffy. Beat in the liqueur, 1 tablespoon at a time, then stir in the chopped pecans. One at a time, pinch off about 1 tablespoon of the mixture and roll it between the palms of your hands until it forms a ball about 1 inch in diameter. Place the balls on a baking sheet lined with wax paper and refrigerate for 30 minutes.

2. Meanwhile, in the top of a double boiler over hot, not simmering, water, melt the white chocolate, stirring until smooth. Remove from the heat and let rest for about 10 minutes, until the chocolate is cool but still fluid.

3. Remove the candies from the refrigerator Spear each candy with a small skewer and dip in the melted chocolate, coating thoroughly, then return to the wax paper. When all of the candies have been coated with chocolate, refrigerate them again for at least 2 hours before serving.

KITCHEN NOTE: *You have to be careful when melting chocolate. If the heat is too high, the chocolate can easily scorch; if you cover the pan, the moisture that condenses on the lid can drip back into the chocolate, causing it to "seize" or stiffen. For safety's sake, melt the chocolate in a double boiler over hot, but not boiling, water; remove the top pan when the chocolate is at least half melted, and then stir it, off the heat, until it is completely melted.*

CANDIED CRANBERRIES

MAKES 2 CUPS

2 CUPS CRANBERRIES
4 CUPS SUGAR

1 CUP WATER
PINCH OF CREAM OF TARTAR

1. With a trussing needle or a small skewer, pierce each cranberry completely through. Set the berries aside.

2. In a medium saucepan, combine 3 cups of the sugar, the water, and the cream of tartar. Stirring constantly, cook over medium heat until the sugar dissolves. Raise the heat, let the syrup come to a boil, and cook briskly, uncovered and undisturbed, for about 5 minutes more, or until the syrup reaches a temperature of 220° on a candy thermometer. Remove the pan from the heat and gently stir the cranberries into the syrup, turning them about with a spoon until the berries are evenly coated. Set aside at room temperature for at least 12 hours, preferably overnight.

3. Stirring gently, bring the cranberries and syrup to a simmer over moderate heat. Then drain the berries in a colander set over a bowl and return the syrup to the saucepan.

4. Bring the syrup to a boil over high heat and cook briskly, uncovered and undisturbed, until it reaches a temperature of 250° on a candy thermometer, or until a few drops spooned into water immediately form a firm but still slightly pliable ball.

5. Remove the pan from the heat, drop the berries into the syrup, and stir gently until they are thoroughly coated and glistening. With a slotted spoon, arrange the berries in 1 layer on a long strip of wax paper. Discard the remaining syrup. Let the berries cool to lukewarm; if pools of syrup collect around any of the berries, carefully move the berries to a clean part of the paper.

6. Two or three at a time, roll the berries in the remaining cup of sugar and transfer them to fresh wax paper. Cool the berries completely to room temperature before serving.

ALMOND-AND-PISTACHIO CANDY

MAKES 2 DOZEN

1 QUART MILK

1 CUP SUGAR

1 CUP GROUND ALMONDS

1 CUP GROUND PISTACHIOS

1 TABLESPOON BUTTER, AT ROOM
  TEMPERATURE

½ TEASPOON ALMOND EXTRACT

1. Grease an 8-inch pie pan.

2. In a large saucepan, bring the milk to a boil over high heat. Reduce the heat to medium and, stirring frequently, cook for about 35 minutes, or until the milk thickens to the consistency of heavy cream. Add the sugar and stir for 10 minutes. Add the ground almonds and pistachios and continue stirring for 10 minutes. Add the butter and cook for another 5 to 10 minutes, stirring, until the mixture is thick enough to draw away from the sides of the pan in a solid mass.

3. Remove the pan from the heat and stir in the almond extract. Pour the candy into the prepared pie pan, spreading and smoothing it with a spatula. Let the candy cool for 30 minutes or so, then cut it into 24 small squares or diamonds. It will harden to the consistency of fudge as it cools further.

WALNUT-HONEY CANDY

MAKES 2 DOZEN

1 POUND WALNUTS OR ALMONDS,
FINELY CHOPPED

2 CUPS HONEY
7 TABLESPOONS SUGAR

1. Preheat the oven to 350°. Spread the walnuts in a single layer on a baking sheet and toast them in the oven for 8 to 10 minutes, turning them from time to time. Watch carefully for any sign of burning.

2. In a medium saucepan, combine the honey and sugar and, stirring constantly, bring to a boil over high heat. When the syrup reaches 220° on a candy thermometer, lower the heat and stir in the nuts. Stirring often, cook 15 minutes.

3. Line a 9-inch pie pan with foil, then brush the inside with cold water and pour in the nut mixture. Smooth the top and set aside, uncovered, to cool. When the candy is firm, dip the pan into hot water and invert a flat plate on top. Grasping the 2 firmly together, turn over; the candy should slide out in 1 piece. With a knife dipped in hot water, cut the candy into diamond shapes.

VARIATION: *A sesame-seed version of this candy is popular in the Middle East. Use toasted sesame seeds, following the directions in Step 1 but checking for doneness after just 5 minutes.*

ALMOND PENUCHE

MAKES 4 DOZEN

2 CUPS LIGHT BROWN SUGAR
2 CUPS GRANULATED SUGAR
2 CUPS LIGHT CREAM

½ TEASPOON VANILLA EXTRACT
1 CUP CHOPPED ALMONDS

1. In a large saucepan, combine the brown sugar, granulated sugar, and cream over high heat and bring to a boil. Let the mixture cook, uncovered and undisturbed, until the candy reaches a temperature of 238° on a candy thermometer, or until a few drops spooned into ice water immediately form a soft but compact ball. Watch the candy carefully and when it begins to bubble up in the pan, reduce the heat for a few moments. If sugar crystals appear around the inside of the pan, brush them back into the candy with a pastry brush that has been lightly moistened with water.

2. Remove the pan from the heat and let the candy cool for about 5 minutes. Meanwhile, generously grease the bottom and sides of an 8 x 6-inch baking dish.

3. When the candy has cooled slightly, beat it with a wooden spoon until it is thick enough to hold its shape almost solidly in the spoon. Beat in the vanilla and almonds, then pour the mixture into the prepared pan, spreading it and smoothing the top with a spoon or spatula. Cool to room temperature, then cut the candy into 1-inch squares.

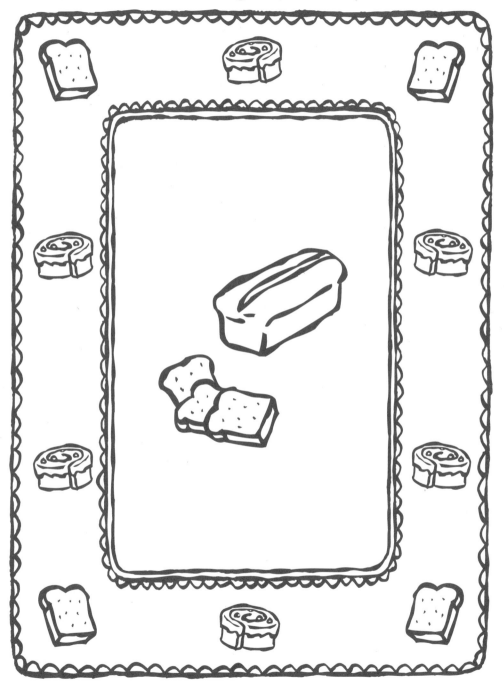

DATE NUT BREAD

2 CUPS FLOUR

1 TABLESPOON BAKING POWDER

1 TEASPOON BAKING SODA

¼ TEASPOON SALT

4 TABLESPOONS BUTTER, AT ROOM
TEMPERATURE

⅓ CUP PACKED BROWN SUGAR

1 EGG

1 TEASPOON VANILLA EXTRACT

1 CUP PEAR NECTAR

1 CUP CHOPPED DATES

1 CUP COARSELY CHOPPED PECANS

1 TABLESPOON GRATED ORANGE ZEST

1. Preheat the oven to 375°. Grease and flour a 9 x 5-inch loaf pan.

2. In a small bowl, stir together the flour, baking powder, baking soda, and salt.

3. In a large bowl, cream the butter and sugar until light and fluffy. Beat in the egg and vanilla. Add half of the flour mixture, then, alternating between the 2, add the pear nectar and the remaining flour mixture, beating well after each addition. Stir in the dates, pecans, and orange zest.

4. Spread the batter evenly in the prepared pan. Rap the pan once on the counter to remove any air pockets. Bake for 50 to 55 minutes, or until the bread is golden and shrinks from the sides of the pan, and a toothpick inserted into the center of the loaf comes out clean.

5. Let the loaf cool in the pan on a rack, then turn it out onto the rack to cool completely before slicing.

CRANBERRY ALMOND BREAD

MAKES ONE 9-INCH LOAF

2 CUPS FLOUR

¾ CUP SUGAR

2 TEASPOONS BAKING POWDER

½ TEASPOON SALT

¾ CUP MILK

6 TABLESPOONS BUTTER, MELTED

1 EGG, LIGHTLY BEATEN

1 TABLESPOON GRATED ORANGE ZEST

1 TEASPOON ALMOND EXTRACT

1 CUP FRESH OR FROZEN CRANBERRIES

1 CUP SLICED ALMONDS

1. Preheat the oven to 325°. Grease and flour a 9 x 5-inch loaf pan.

2. In a large bowl, blend the flour, sugar, baking powder, and salt. In another bowl, combine the milk, butter, egg, orange zest, and almond extract. Add the wet ingredients to the dry ingredients and stir until no streaks of flour remain. Fold in the cranberries and the almonds.

3. Pour the batter into the prepared pan and spread evenly. Rap the pan once or twice on the counter to remove any air pockets. Bake for 1 hour and 10 minutes, or until the top is golden and a toothpick inserted into the center of the bread comes out clean. Cool the bread in the pan for 10 minutes and then turn it out onto a rack to cool completely before slicing.

KITCHEN NOTE: *Cranberries are most plentiful in the fall and early winter. You can freeze them right in their original bags for up to a year, so if you pick up a few extra bags at the height of the season, you can enjoy this berry-studded bread all year round. A 12-ounce bag of cranberries yields about 3 cups.*

GOLDEN PUMPKIN BREAD

MAKES ONE 9-INCH LOAF

1½ CUPS FLOUR

½ CUP YELLOW CORNMEAL

1 TEASPOON BAKING POWDER

1 TEASPOON CINNAMON

1 TEASPOON GROUND GINGER

1 TEASPOON NUTMEG

½ TEASPOON SALT

1 STICK BUTTER, AT ROOM
  TEMPERATURE

⅔ CUP SUGAR

2 EGGS

1 CUP CANNED PUMPKIN

1 CUP CHOPPED PECANS

1 CUP RAISINS

1. Preheat the oven to 350°. Grease and flour a 9 x 5-inch loaf pan.

2. In a medium bowl, combine the flour, cornmeal, baking powder, cinnamon, ginger, nutmeg, and salt.

3. In a large bowl, cream the butter and sugar. Beat in the eggs, 1 at a time, beating well after each addition. Stir in the pumpkin until thoroughly combined, then gradually add the flour mixture, beating just until incorporated; do not overbeat. Stir in the pecans and raisins.

4. Spread the batter evenly in the prepared pan. Rap the pan once on the counter to remove any air pockets. Bake for 50 to 60 minutes, or until the bread shrinks from the sides of the pan and a toothpick inserted into the center of the loaf comes out clean.

5. Let the loaf cool in the pan on a rack for 10 minutes, then turn it out onto the rack to cool completely.

LEMON TEA LOAF

2 CUPS FLOUR

2 TEASPOONS BAKING POWDER

½ TEASPOON BAKING SODA

½ TEASPOON SALT

2 STICKS BUTTER, AT ROOM
TEMPERATURE

¾ CUP SUGAR

3 EGGS

2 TEASPOONS GRATED LEMON ZEST

¼ CUP FRESH LEMON JUICE

1. Preheat the oven to 350°. Grease and flour a 9 x 5-inch loaf pan.

2. In a medium bowl, stir together the flour, baking powder, baking soda, and salt; set aside.

3. In a large bowl, cream the butter and sugar. Beat in the eggs, 1 at a time, beating well after each addition. Beat in the lemon zest and juice. Gradually add the flour mixture, stirring just until incorporated.

4. Spread the batter evenly in the prepared pan. Rap the pan once on the counter to remove any air pockets. Bake for 55 to 60 minutes, or until the top of the loaf is golden, the bread shrinks from the sides of the pan, and a toothpick inserted into the center comes out clean.

5. Let the loaf cool in the pan on a rack, then turn it out onto the rack to cool completely before slicing.

KITCHEN NOTE: *If you have any of this delicately fragrant loaf left over (and that's not too likely), treat yourself to a special breakfast: Slice and lightly toast the bread and serve with raspberry jam.*

Sweet Potato Swirl Bread

MAKES ONE 9-INCH LOAF

1¾ CUPS FLOUR

1 TEASPOON BAKING SODA

PINCH OF SALT

1 STICK BUTTER, AT ROOM
  TEMPERATURE

1 CUP LIGHT BROWN SUGAR

2 EGGS

1 TEASPOON VANILLA EXTRACT

1½ CUPS COOKED, PEELED, AND
  MASHED SWEET POTATOES

1 CUP COARSLEY CHOPPED WALNUTS

⅓ CUP COCOA POWDER

1. Preheat the oven to 350°. Grease and flour a 9 x 5-inch loaf pan.

2. In a small bowl, stir together the flour, baking soda, and salt; set aside.

3. In a medium bowl, cream the butter and sugar until light and fluffy. Beat in the eggs, 1 at a time, beating well after each addition, then beat in the vanilla. Stir in the sweet potatoes until thoroughly combined, then gradually add the flour mixture, beating just until incorporated. Stir in the walnuts.

4. Transfer ⅓ of the batter to a small bowl, add the cocoa powder, and stir until blended.

5. Spread the plain batter in the prepared pan, then spread the cocoa batter on top. Swirl a table knife through the batter to marbleize it. Rap the pan once or twice on the counter to remove any air pockets.

6. Bake for 1 to 1¼ hours, or until the bread shrinks from the sides of the pan and a toothpick inserted into the center of the loaf comes out clean.

7. Let the loaf cool in the pan on a rack, then turn it out onto the rack to cool completely before slicing.

KITCHEN NOTE: *Whenever you have leftover sweet potatoes—perhaps after a holiday meal—this is a delicious and novel way to use them. To cook potatoes specifically for this recipe, you have several options. Slow baking is the method that brings out their flavor best. However, if you're pressed for time, either cut the potatoes into chunks and steam them, or pierce the whole potatoes a few times with a fork and cook them in the microwave.*

Raisin Scones

MAKES 1 DOZEN

3 EGGS, LIGHTLY BEATEN
¾ CUP BUTTERMILK
3⅓ CUPS FLOUR
3 TABLESPOONS SUGAR
1 TABLESPOON BAKING POWDER

¼ TEASPOON SALT
1 STICK BUTTER, AT ROOM
  TEMPERATURE
½ CUP GOLDEN RAISINS
½ CUP COARSELY CHOPPED WALNUTS

1. Preheat the oven to 425°. Lightly grease a large baking sheet.

2. In a small bowl, stir together the eggs and buttermilk; set aside.

3. In a large bowl, stir together the flour, sugar, baking powder, and salt. With a pastry blender or 2 knives, cut the butter into the flour mixture until it is coarse crumbs. Stir in the raisins and walnuts, and make a well in the center. Pour in the egg-buttermilk mixture and stir until blended. Continue stirring the mixture until it forms a soft dough that can be gathered into a ball.

4. Place the dough on a lightly floured surface and knead it until smooth, 3 to 5 minutes. With a lightly floured rolling pin, roll out the dough to a ¼-inch-thick round, 9 to 10 inches in diameter.

5. Using a knife dipped in flour, cut the dough into 12 wedges. Transfer the wedges to the prepared baking sheet and bake for 18 to 20 minutes, or until the scones are puffed and golden brown.

Cinnamon Sticky Buns

MAKES 14

1 CUP MILK

2 STICKS BUTTER, AT ROOM
   TEMPERATURE

⅓ CUP GRANULATED SUGAR

¼ CUP LUKEWARM WATER

1 PACKAGE ACTIVE DRY YEAST

ABOUT 5½ CUPS FLOUR

½ TEASPOON SALT

1¼ CUPS DARK BROWN SUGAR

1 TABLESPOON CINNAMON

½ CUP DARK CORN SYRUP

1. In a small saucepan, scald the milk over medium heat. Add 4 tablespoons of the butter and the granulated sugar, and stir until the butter is melted and the sugar is dissolved.

2. Place the water in a small bowl and sprinkle the yeast over it. Stir in a pinch of granulated sugar and let stand until the yeast begins to foam, about 5 minutes.

3. In a large bowl, stir together 4¾ cups of the flour and the salt, and make a well in the center. Pour in the milk mixture and the yeast mixture, and stir until a soft dough forms.

4. Transfer the dough to a lightly floured surface and knead it until smooth, adding up to ½ cup more flour. Place the dough in a large greased bowl. Cover with a slightly dampened cloth and set in a warm place to rise until doubled in size, 45 minutes to 1 hour.

5. Meanwhile, lightly grease two 9-inch cake pans. In a small bowl, stir together ¾ cup of the brown sugar and the cinnamon; set aside.

6. In a large saucepan, warm the corn syrup, 1 stick of butter, and ½ cup brown sugar over low heat, stirring constantly, until the butter is melted and the sugar is dissolved. Pour the glaze into the bottoms of the prepared pans.

7. Punch the dough down, then transfer it to a lightly floured surface. Roll out the dough to a 12 x 21-inch rectangle. Brush the dough with the remaining 4 tablespoons butter, then sprinkle it with the sugar-cinnamon filling. Starting at 1 long side, roll the dough jelly-roll fashion. Cut the roll into fourteen 1½-inch slices. Place 6 slices in a circle around the edge of each pan and 1 in the center of each. Set aside, uncovered, in a warm place to rise for 25 minutes, or until doubled in size.

8. Preheat the oven to 375°. Bake for 25 to 30 minutes, or until the buns are golden brown. Immediately run the tip of a knife around the edges of the pans, then invert the buns onto serving plates. Serve warm.

jAm PinWHEELS

MAKES 20

¾ CUP PLUS 1 TABLESPOON MILK

1 PACKAGE ACTIVE DRY YEAST

1 EGG, LIGHTLY BEATEN, PLUS 1 EGG
YOLK

4 TABLESPOONS BUTTER, MELTED

⅓ CUP SUGAR

ABOUT 2½ CUPS FLOUR

¼ TEASPOON SALT

ABOUT ¼ CUP JAM

1. In a small saucepan, heat ¼ cup of the milk over medium heat to almost boiling. Remove the pan from the heat and let the milk cool to lukewarm. Sprinkle the yeast over the milk and stir until dissolved.

2. In a small bowl, combine ½ cup of milk, the whole egg, butter, and sugar.

3. In a large bowl, combine 2 cups of the flour and the salt, and make a well in the center. Pour in the yeast mixture and the milk mixture, and stir until a soft dough forms.

4. Transfer the dough to a lightly floured surface and knead it until smooth and elastic, about 10 minutes, adding up to ½ cup more flour if necessary. Form the dough into a ball and place it in a large greased bowl. Cover the bowl with a slightly dampened kitchen towel and set it in a warm place to rise until doubled in bulk, 45 minutes to 1 hour.

5. Lightly grease a baking sheet. Punch the dough down, then transfer it to a lightly floured surface and knead for 2 minutes. Roll out the dough to a rectangle roughly 15 x 12 inches. Cut the dough into twenty 3-inch squares. Transfer the squares of dough to the prepared baking sheet. Make diagonal cuts from the corners of each square to within about ¾ inch of the center.

6. Place ½ teaspoon of jam in the center of each square. Fold every other point toward the center (the dough should not completely cover the jam) to form pinwheels, and seal the points with a drop of water. Tuck the last point under the pastry.

7. Set the pastries aside, uncovered, in a warm, draft-free place to rise for 20 minutes.

8. Preheat the oven to 375°. In a small bowl, beat the egg yolk with the remaining tablespoon milk. Brush the pastries with the glaze and bake for 15 to 20 minutes, or until golden brown and firm. Let the pastries cool on the baking sheet for 2 to 3 minutes, then transfer them to a rack to cool completely.

Apple-Filled Crisscross

MAKES TWO 9-INCH LOAVES

¼ CUP LUKEWARM WATER

1 PACKAGE ACTIVE DRY YEAST

¼ CUP GRANULATED SUGAR

⅓ CUP SOUR CREAM

2 TABLESPOONS LUKEWARM MILK

1 EGG, LIGHTLY BEATEN

½ TEASPOON VANILLA EXTRACT

ABOUT 3 CUPS FLOUR

¼ TEASPOON SALT

6 TABLESPOONS BUTTER, MELTED

1 SMALL APPLE, COARSELY CHOPPED

¼ CUP RAISINS

3 TABLESPOONS FRESH BREAD CRUMBS

¼ CUP CHOPPED WALNUTS

2 TABLESPOONS LIGHT BROWN SUGAR

½ TEASPOON CINNAMON

1 TEASPOON FRESH LEMON JUICE

1. Place the water in a small bowl and sprinkle the yeast and a pinch of sugar over it. Let stand until the yeast foams, about 5 minutes.

2. In a small bowl, combine the granulated sugar, the sour cream, milk, egg, and vanilla.

3. In a large bowl, stir together 2½ cups of flour and the salt. Stir in the yeast mixture and the milk mixture. Add the butter and mix until well blended. On a lightly floured surface, knead the dough until smooth, adding up to ½ cup more flour. Place the dough in a large greased bowl. Cover with a dampened towel and set in a warm place to rise until doubled in size, 45 minutes to 1 hour.

4. Meanwhile, in a medium bowl, combine the apple, raisins, bread crumbs, walnuts, brown sugar, cinnamon, and lemon juice.

5. Grease and flour 2 baking sheets. Punch down the dough. On a lightly floured surface, knead the dough for about 5 minutes. Roll out the dough to an 18 x 8-inch rectangle, then cut it into 9 x 8-inch rectangles. Place each rectangle on a prepared baking sheet.

6. Spread half of the apple filling in a 2-inch-wide strip down the center of each piece of dough, leaving a border of about ½ inch at the top and bottom. Starting ½ inch from the filling, make diagonal cuts ½ inch apart, from the filling out to the edges of the dough, on both sides. Crisscross the strips over the filling. Tuck the last 2 strips under and press firmly to seal. Set the loaves aside, uncovered, in a warm place to rise for 20 minutes.

7. Preheat the oven to 375°. Bake each loaf separately for 15 minutes, or until golden.

SWEDISH CHERRY TWIST

MAKES ONE 16-INCH TWIST

¼ CUP LUKEWARM WATER

1 PACKAGE ACTIVE DRY YEAST

¾ CUP LUKEWARM MILK

4 TABLESPOONS UNSALTED BUTTER, MELTED

1 TEASPOON SALT

⅓ CUP GRANULATED SUGAR

1 EGG, LIGHTLY BEATEN

3 TO 3½ CUPS FLOUR

1 EGG YOLK, LIGHTLY BEATEN WITH 1 TABLESPOON MILK

¼ CUP ALMONDS, COARSELY CHOPPED

¼ CUP LIGHT BROWN SUGAR

1 TEASPOON CINNAMON

4 CANDIED CHERRIES, HALVED

1. Pour the water into a small bowl and sprinkle the yeast and a pinch of granulated sugar over it. Let stand for 2 to 3 minutes, then stir well. Set in a warm place for 10 minutes, or until bubbly and doubled in volume.

2. In a large bowl, combine the milk, butter, salt, granulated sugar, and egg, and stir until well blended. Add 3 cups of flour, 1 cup at a time, and continue to stir until a soft dough forms. Place the dough on a lightly floured surface and knead until the dough is shiny and elastic, adding up to ½ cup more flour. Place the dough in a large greased bowl. Cover the bowl with a dampened kitchen towel and put it in a warm place for about 45 minutes, or until the dough doubles in bulk. Grease a large baking sheet.

3. Punch the dough down, then place on a lightly floured surface. Cut the dough in half and shape each half into a cylinder about 18 inches long. Place the cylinders on the prepared baking sheet and pinch the tops together so that the cylinders form a narrow V. Shape the dough into a twist, about 14 inches long. Set aside to rise for 45 minutes, or until doubled in bulk.

4. Preheat the oven to 375°. With a pastry brush, coat the twist with the combined egg yolk and milk. Mix the almonds, brown sugar, and cinnamon, and sprinkle over the top. Set the candied cherry halves in 2 rows along the length of the twist. Bake for 25 minutes, or until golden brown. Turn the twist out onto a rack to cool.

Buttermilk Coffee Cake

SERVES 6 TO 8

2 CUPS FLOUR

1½ TEASPOONS BAKING POWDER

1 CUP LIGHT BROWN SUGAR

1½ STICKS UNSALTED BUTTER, CUT
INTO PIECES

⅔ CUP BUTTERMILK

1 EGG, LIGHTLY BEATEN

½ CUP FINELY CHOPPED PECANS OR
ALMONDS

1 TEASPOON GROUND CINNAMON

½ CUP CURRANTS

1. Preheat the oven to 425°. Grease and flour the bottom and sides of a 9-inch round cake pan.

2. In a large bowl, combine the flour, baking powder, sugar, and butter, and rub them together with your fingertips until the mixture is fine crumbs. Set aside ½ cup of the mixture to be used for the topping.

3. Into the remaining mixture, gradually stir the buttermilk, egg, pecans, cinnamon, and currants. When the ingredients are well combined and the batter is smooth, pour it into the prepared pan and sprinkle the top evenly with the reserved crumb mixture.

4. Bake the cake for 15 minutes, then reduce the oven temperature to 375°. Bake for an additional 20 to 25 minutes, or until a small knife inserted into the center of the cake comes out clean. Serve the coffee cake warm or at room temperature.

SUBSTITUTION: *If you have no buttermilk on hand, you can substitute plain yogurt. Or, place 2 teaspoons of white vinegar or lemon juice in a liquid measuring cup and add enough regular milk to measure ⅔ cup. Stir, then let stand for 5 minutes.*

BLUEBERRY COFFEE CAKE

SERVES 6 TO 8

1¼ CUPS FLOUR

1 TEASPOON BAKING POWDER

½ TEASPOON BAKING SODA

¼ TEASPOON SALT

1 STICK PLUS 3 TABLESPOONS BUTTER,
    AT ROOM TEMPERATURE

⅔ CUP LIGHT BROWN SUGAR

1 EGG

¼ CUP BUTTERMILK

1 TEASPOON VANILLA EXTRACT

½ TEASPOON CINNAMON

3 CUPS FRESH OR FROZEN BLUEBERRIES

2 TEASPOONS POWDERED SUGAR

1. Preheat the oven to 350°. Grease an 8-inch round cake pan and line the bottom with wax paper. Grease the wax paper, then flour the pan.

2. In a medium bowl, stir together 1 cup of the flour, the baking powder, baking soda, and salt.

3. In a large bowl, cream 1 stick of the butter and the brown sugar. Beat in the egg, buttermilk, and vanilla. Gradually add the flour mixture, beating well after each addition. Spread the batter evenly in the prepared pan; set aside.

4. In a small bowl, mix the remaining ¼ cup of flour and the cinnamon. With a pastry blender or 2 knives, cut in the remaining butter until the mixture is coarse crumbs.

5. Spread the blueberries evenly over the cake layer, then sprinkle the topping over them. Bake for 1 hour, or until the topping is golden and beginning to brown around the edges.

6. Let the cake cool in the pan on a rack for 30 minutes.

7. Run the tip of a knife around the edges of the pan to loosen the cake, then turn it out onto a plate. Immediately invert the cake onto a serving plate. Dust the top with the powdered sugar and serve warm.

INDEX